REBUILDING

NEHEMIAH

REBUILDING
NEHEMIAH:
A JOURNEY BACK TO WHOLENESS

JOE BUCK IV

XULON PRESS

Xulon Press
2301 Lucien Way #415
Maitland, FL 32751
407.339.4217
www.xulonpress.com

Paperback ISBN-13: 978-1-6628-0798-5
eBook ISBN-13: 978-1-6628-0799-2

DEDICATION

To God be all the glory and honor and praise!
I thank God for giving me this message and for being patient,
forgiving my delayed obedience.
May God bless each reader and speak life into those
broken down walls we call the body, mind, and soul.

TABLE OF CONTENTS

Dedication v

Preface ix

Chapter 1   Who You Are 1

Chapter 2:   Know What You Are Getting Into. 17

Chapter 3:   The Way to Getting Better 41

Chapter 4   Do What It Takes. 59

Chapter 5   Get to Work 85

Chapter 6   Defeat Resistance. 97

Chapter 7   Make a Lasting Change. 115

Chapter 8   Watch Your Step. 129

Chapter 9   "Focus, Daniel-san. Focus." 145

Chapter 10   Who's With Me?! 171

Chapter 11   Best Laid Plans. 183

Appendix   exerceo divina 207

Acknowledgements 227

Endnotes 229

PREFACE

ONE OF THE MOST sensory accounts in the Bible comes from the prophet Ezekiel in the book of the same name. The context for his prophecy is ours for this book: significant issues. The kingdoms of Israel and Judah have fallen. Israel is long gone thanks to the Assyrians. They wiped the Northern Tribes off the map two hundred years before the Babylonians showed up to finish the job. For 30 months they laid siege to Jerusalem to crush the last defenses of the Southern Tribes. They were decimated. While the Northern Tribes became forever *The Lost Tribes of Israel*, the remnant of the Southern Tribes were exiled to Babylon.

There is no hope for God's people. They gave up on God long ago, and God has given them what they wanted, life without Him. Ezekiel is prophesying to God's people about hope. Even though there is a great deal of judgment in his testimony, there is hope. The strongest message of hope comes in Ezekiel 37 in a valley of dry bones.

God picked up Ezekiel, and He set him down in an open field full of human carcasses. Think about an old photo of a Civil War battle, with bodies as far as you can see. The bloodshed was so fierce, you can hardly walk through the field because of how many bodies are there and how close the combat was. Now, imagine the bodies were stripped of their clothes and left to rot. Eventually, time and the sun would wash them white. There would be bones upon bones. This is where God dropped Ezekiel.

God gave Ezekiel perspective on just how bad things were for God's people. There was no coming back from this…how could they? As a nation, they were in shambles. They were defeated, and their temple was gone as well as their treasury. They cried out to God: "Our bones are dried up, and our hope is gone, there's nothing left of us" (Ezek. 37:11b, MSG). Judah was a big pile of bones.

Just when all seemed lost, God had a message of redemption—rebuilding from the ground up. God told Ezekiel what to say, and he said it. Ezekiel told the bones to come together. He spoke God's words to create muscle and soft tissue—ligaments and tendons. Organs were created and systems were connected. He spoke skin onto the bodies, but there was no more movement. The action stopped, and he waited for God to speak.

God told Ezekiel to call on His breath—The Spirit of God—to finish the job. Ezekiel spoke God's words and the Spirit moved. The bodies were invigorated with life as God breathed into them. All of them. Every body on that lifeless, desolate field came to life. They stood right where they were, and it was amazing. It was God's nation…God's people alive and on their feet.

Ezekiel was so excited, he could hardly contain himself. He ran to the people to tell them where God had taken him and what he had seen. There was hope after all. Ezekiel gave them God's message:

> I'll dig up your graves and bring you out alive—O
> my people! Then I'll take you straight to the land of
> Israel. When I dig up graves and bring you out as
> My people, you'll realize that I am God. I'll breathe

my life into you and you'll live. Then I'll lead you straight back to your land and you'll realize that I am God. I've said it and I'll do it. God's decree (Ezek. 37:12-14, MSG).

God's message—His decree—was delivered: there was always hope for a rebuilding effort.

That message was not just meant for the nations of Judah and Israel. God is in the *amazing* business, and there is always hope. We know deep down that no matter how bad things may get or appear, God is all-powerful and cannot be stopped. Superpower after superpower has come and gone, but God is eternal and victorious. A physical or mental injury may put us on the ground… and even in a hole, but God is in the *amazing* business.

You may feel just like the remnant of God's chosen people. Repairing a damaged home is never easy, and neither is rebuilding your life going to be easy. When there is a problem in our lives, we have to do something. If your house was missing a window or a tree has fallen on top of it, you kind of have to do something. Who in their right mind would ignore the hole in the roof as the rain soaks the floor? Who would try to explain away the cold wind blowing through your house in the cold of winter? We do not do that, because we know better. Why do we do that with our own bodies?

You and I have problems. None of us is immune to struggle. Our minds, bodies, and souls are complicated, and how they work together is even more so. But, when we have a problem, we need to do something about it.

One question you hear a lot around home repairs is about the structure of a house. Every house that has some years on it will have a story to tell. Some are in better condition than others. Some had a tougher time than others. People always want to know when renovation work is needed, *Does the house have good bones?* It is another way of asking if this house is worth the effort. It will take some money, supplies, and sweat to bring this house back. Is it worth it?

The number one reason we do not do something about the broken roof in our lives or the missing window is we do not have the time needed. We are busy…too busy. We are so busy we decide to ignore the rain in our living room and the icy breeze blowing through the house. We cannot afford to do that for very long, no matter how busy we are.

If you are reading this book, we may have a chance to do something amazing. You are a child of God. Either you are a follower of Jesus or you could be. Either way, He loves you, and Jesus is in the *amazing* business. You have good bones. You may be heavier than you…or the doctor…want you to be. Your blood work may be less than ideal. The warning signs may be there that something has to change, right now. You may be coming back from an injury or a surgery or an accident. Things can seem hopeless. You may think, *I do not have it in me to do this.* Do not believe the lies you or others are telling you, because you have good bones.

Those problems you feel have gotten too big or are too daunting, well…they are not either. You can conquer them with God's strength. You cannot do it on your own, but with God, all things are possible. If God is calling you to a healthier lifestyle, all you have to do is respond. God has already fought the battle and is just waiting on you to do your part.

On your best day, you may feel like there is a glimmer of hope; maybe today is the day for progress. On your worst day, it may feel like you are already in a hole, six feet under. Hang onto that rope that is your glimmer of hope. It may start off as a strand of dental floss, but it will grow with God's strength. God will turn that version of hope into a chord that is threaded with titanium, incapable of breaking.

This book is built on hope. This book is filled with hope. Our God is the source of all hope. Life-change comes through the power of God, first, but we must do our part as well. It will not be easy, but it *will* be worth it. There is life in those dry bones…young, tired, old, broken…whatever. Rely on God, and you will see and do amazing things.

CHAPTER 1

WHO YOU ARE

WHEN WE ARE BROKEN, we are broken. That term does not allow for being a little broken. Just as you can't be a little pregnant or a little committed. Whether it is your mind, your body, or your soul, being broken is a horrible thing.

There is a sort of clarity that must come from that state. When we realize we exist in that condition, only then is there the semblance of the beginning of recovery. When our bodies are broken, when our souls have been devoured, and when our minds are splintered, there must be reconstruction. There must be repair, but that can only begin when we realize where we are and who we want to be. So, to say it in a better, more succinct manner, we must realize who we are in our state and our current position and establish a goal to which we can strive: who we need to be.

In Nehemiah 1:1-3 (NASB), we see a dire situation:

> "The words of Nehemiah the son of Hacaliah. Now it happened in the month Chislev, *in* the twentieth year, while I was in Susa the capitol, that Hanani, one of my brothers, and some men from Judah came; and I asked them concerning the Jews who had escaped *and* had survived the captivity, and

about Jerusalem. They said to me, "The remnant there in the province who survived the captivity are in great distress and reproach, and the wall of Jerusalem is broken down and its gates are burned with fire."

Nehemiah finds out in the first three verses from one of his brothers and fellow survivors the state of his home. He hears the walls are broken down, and he also hears the gates have been burned up. The news that he hears from credible sources tears him apart—destroying him. He realizes how bad things have gotten.

The Babylonians had conquered the Jews—they had decimated them as a people. They destroyed their homeland and they removed the elite—the smartest, the brightest, and the potential for rejuvenation. They took the best that Judea had to offer. The Babylonians left no doubt that they were the conquerors and the Jews had been conquered. They not only took the best the Jews had to offer but they harnessed that ability and transplanted them to the center of their power and government and administration. Thus, they utilized the most talented and gifted of God's chosen people, and they prospered from their abilities.

Years ago, I remember when Major League Baseball decided to expand by adding two new teams to the National League. They revised a policy on how you start a brand-new team with no talent and no players on the roster. They allowed the new teams and their scouts and general manager to pick players from other teams to build their team. They scouted the teams and decided who they wanted to steal—and some teams couldn't afford to lose the talent they were required to lose for the expansion. Each of the existing teams was allowed to protect 15 players on their 40-man roster.

There was a draft with three rounds and out of that the Colorado Rockies and the Florida Marlins were born. In all, 72 players were drafted.

The two teams had differing strategies: the Rockies decided to draft the young prospects while the Marlins decided to go with the veteran players. In their first full season in 1993 they both finished next to last in their divisions. But just two years later the Rockies made the playoffs, which was a record for making the playoffs quickest after an expansion. Meanwhile, the Marlins used many of their players to trade for other players they really wanted. Their team won the World Series in 1997. Talent matters any way that you can get it, and you need talented people committed to a purpose.

Nehemiah's generation grew up in exile…in captivity. All they ever knew was Babylon. It was a real example of out of sight, out of mind. He was not aware of how bad things had gotten. Upon hearing that Jerusalem was decimated—unprotected from any marauders or nomads that wanted to dwell there—he committed himself to God's attention and intervention.

During the exile he was left to his own imagination, to contemplate how things were going back in Israel. He could not fully conceive of how bad things really were. Nehemiah was oblivious to the state of affairs, and then he had a reality check. It is only then that Nehemiah can begin the process of rebuilding even as just an initial inkling of potential. And not just rebuilding his homeland, but rebuilding his identity as a Jew—as one of the chosen people of God.

I had never known what it was to have my body broken. I certainly knew what it was to have my mind or my soul damaged, but my body had not been broken. But early on the morning of July

17, 2013, one minute or two before 8 o'clock on a beautiful sunny day with blue skies and high visibility, it happened. I was biking on the side of the road on the painted line when I was hit. I did not know what had happened. Before I knew it there was a collision and I was no longer on my bicycle.

I was struck from behind by a car going 40 to 50 mph. The driver hit me with the front of her car as she had somehow veered over, distracted by something. She had only been on that particular stretch of road for about a tenth of a mile when she hit me. The sun was behind us, so there was no glare or blind spot from the sun. I was wearing a white shirt, but she still never saw me. She drove through me with no awareness that I was even there; she just saw a white flash.

I was cycling at about 20 to 22 mph. The impact sent me and my bicycle into the air. I was cleated onto my bike, which became a problem as my bike and I went in different directions. My left foot was nearly ripped off of my leg. I slammed into her windshield cracking it with my head and helmet, which was broken in the collision. I then ricocheted off the windshield and "flew" (as one witness described the accident) some 15 feet and landed rather rudely on the shoulder of the road and tumbled to a stop in the ditch. While I was tumbling I said, "Oh, no. Oh, no." My wild ride was over, but that was just the beginning of a very long day.

Those first few moments on the side of the road were the scariest. I was in a great deal of pain instantly, but I couldn't breathe and my mouth was full of blood. That is when I had the very real thought that I was going to die on the side of the road. All those years of cycling and it finally happened—I was hit by a car and now I'm going to die alone on the side of the road. It was scary. It was a reflex to the shock of the trauma and its aftermath, but the fear was fleeting.

As soon as that instance started it was over. God was there. In fact, God was with me throughout this entire experience. I experienced an odd calm in light of the seriousness of the accident. I had an assurance that only God could provide. It was not theoretical; it was real in that moment and throughout the rest of that day and the days to follow. I had an awareness that I had survived that accident because God was not done with me yet. Later, the Georgia State Patrol and the head of the Medical College of Georgia (MCG) Trauma Center explained to me, it doesn't end like this. There is usually significant head trauma, paralysis, or death. I was alive for a reason, but there was still much work to be done.

As the shock of the accident waned, my lungs and core muscles relaxed. I was able to take a breath and I felt my lungs fill with air. I realized that I wasn't bleeding out, that my mouth was full of blood from some unknown injury. So I started to spit blood out of my mouth, and I was able to breath. Then I checked my teeth to see if they were still in my head, and then all I could think about was pain.

At this point I was not scared, I was just hurting. The driver who hit me did pull over after she heard me bounce off of her car, and all she could say to the truck drivers who pulled over to help was, "I never saw him, I never saw him." She just remembers seeing the white flash in the air. She hurried up to me and was rather hysterical and asked if there is something she could do. I said, "Just get help; I need help; please get help." So she talked with one of the truck drivers who had a cell phone and they called 911 and alerted an ambulance to come get me. The hospital was maybe a mile away, so I figured, hopefully, that meant the ambulance would be there quickly, which it was.

The EMTs were there pretty quick, and they began their assessment. They were very thorough and very worried about all of my injuries. Realizing that my back was injured and that my leg was obviously broken in several places, they immobilized me everywhere they could. They put me on a backboard with a neck brace, and they strapped me down, so I was secured. They put my leg in a splint and began to have a conversation about which hospital we should go to.

This was a somewhat comical conversation as I could hear them discussing my injuries while crouching down by my feet. One EMT suggested maybe we could go to the local hospital. To that idea the other EMT said quite loudly, have you seen that leg, he's got to go to MCG in Augusta (now Georgia Regents University Medical Center). (My leg was lacerated as well as extremely swollen already and it appeared to be a compound fracture.) So, they loaded me into the ambulance, and we went to MCG trauma in Augusta.

Nehemiah was broken himself, although he really was not forced to face that reality. He was the cup-bearer, or sommelier to the most powerful king in the world—an expert in grapes and the fruit of the vine who would ensure the king drank only the finest and tastiest wines. His life was pretty good. His biggest priorities were making sure the king was not poisoned by the wine and that the vintage of the wine was the best it could be.

Nehemiah would have dressed well and been cared for as a palace regular. But the role of cup-bearer was not who he was created to be. Nehemiah had a much more important calling and job than serving that king. Nehemiah was soon to find out the King of Heaven needed his services…and not as a cup-bearer.

Nehemiah was confronted with new information: Jerusalem was in ruins. I'm not sure what Nehemiah thought was going on back home, but misinformation must have been prominent. Maybe he heard from the Babylonians that things were good back home. Maybe he just never thought about it until he had to confront the truth as told to him by his brother and friends. They brought an eyewitness account that he had to listen to.

The travellers share their unsettling news—his home was destroyed—and he was troubled by that fact. Spiritually, his relationship with God was not right. I speculate he was so upset because he knew he wasn't doing anything for his people and only looking out for himself. We don't truly know why he *had* to do something; we just know he had to do *something*.

Everyday life can become commonplace, and self-awareness can become a challenging endeavor. This lack of awareness is not always an intentional mistake, but the misconception is still a limitation. Any time a person does not have a true awareness of self, challenges and character flaws can develop into limitations to God's work in this world. Humanity is to work in concert with Jesus: to be fully devoted to Jesus' purpose for his Body. That awareness can be difficult to maintain, but it is a worthwhile endeavor.

Issues around body image are widespread, and problems often emerge because of a misinformed view of one's body. Jesus asked about such a lack of self-awareness in Matthew 7:3: "Why do you see the speck in your neighbor's eye, but do not notice the log in your own eye?" Author David Stoop writes of the way people can struggle with self-awareness. When dealing with the issue of perfectionism, which 84 percent of people do, Stoop suggests two ways to handle the disorder of perfectionism: The inclinations are to overwork to reach the goal or to underachieve, oblivious to the current flawed state. He claims that either of these pursuits is unhealthy and can lead to discouragement and exhaustion.

Stoop explains that perfectionists lose themselves in the ideal and the never-ending struggle to achieve unattainable goals, ending in their unhappiness at best and extreme depression at worst. Alternatively, perfectionists can also reject the pursuit of the ideal and limit their effort and embrace a false image of who they are. They no longer see themselves as they truly are. Rather, they see the ideal image of themselves when they look in the mirror.[1]

What they think they look like and how they think they are doing can be miles apart from who they truly are. This problem is more prevalent than most would expect, and many no longer see their own degenerative state. They are truly unaware that their health is in a state of disrepair, unknowingly waiting for the arrival of a catastrophic disorder.

While some are oblivious to their fallen state, others have chosen to make decisions that contribute to their unhealth. For example, some elevate food above the place of God thereby manipulating the created order to worship objects that God has given humanity to power their bodies. The first and second commandments state that nothing comes before God, and God's followers are not to make idols out of any of His creation (Exod. 20:2-6). We should only worship God, and we should not let anything take the place of God. Food is repeatedly put before God. In fact, people plan their entire day around what they are going to eat and when they will consume it.

Kenneth L. Barker and John R. Kohlenberger, III describe the first commandment: "You shall not prefer other gods to me."[2] People decide food is a preference ahead of making the decisions they know to be good for them. Others put their job before their physical, mental, and spiritual health by not scheduling time for self-care, making career the idol they worship. The choices people make should be beneficial to their own bodies and to the community of believers working for God's purposes. Barker and Kohlenberger suggest that idolatry, described in this book as the elevation of food, vices, or past-times above the authority of God, is spiritual adultery.[3] People reject God to indulge the evils of another master.

Paul makes a reference to food idolatry in Philippians 3:19. Paul describes those who do not follow Christ: "Their end is destruction; their god is their belly; and their glory is in their shame; their minds are set on earthly things" (NASB). I argue that Paul defines a great number of issues with the term *earthly things*. Our minds are set on idols we can construct and pursuits that we know are not godly or healthy. This Scripture reference, which validates the concern with physical fitness and wellness, contributes to an understanding of the sinfulness of neglecting the body.

Sin is ever present, and sin's connection with abuse and neglect of the body must be recognized for the serious damage it can cause. Maxie Dunnam and Kimberly Dunnam Reisman, in their study of the seven deadly sins, address the sins of gluttony and sloth. Gluttony is described as the "twin brother to lust" because food is the "flesh" that is longed for by the glutton.[4]

Food has become a center of life and quite a money-making endeavor: "The two biggest sellers in bookstores are cookbooks and diet books. The cookbooks tell us how to cook delicious foods; the diet books tell us how not to eat them".[5] Dunnam and Reisman discount the asceticism of St. Francis of Assisi who referred to his body as "Brother Ass" because he saw the body as the servant, as the beast of burden. The authors disregard St. Francis' reference too glibly. Extreme asceticism of the body is not the answer, but the lusts and desires of the world should be harnessed.

The body should serve God and, peripherally, the self. The first step to wellness is to recognize that the beast of burden does not control the feeding; the master does. To achieve the correct equilibrium, we, as the beast of burden, must be trained to serve and fulfill its purpose in support of the Master—God—above all else.

Dunnam and Reisman further contribute to the conversation with their discussion of the sin of sloth. The authors describe this inability to act as laziness, and they ask the reader to consider "the assertion that sloth (laziness) is the attempt to be less than human".[6] Their contention is that sloth—in this book, the choice not to care for the human body with exercise, the spirit through Scripture reading and prayer and the mind through study and education—is a rejection of the Gospel of Jesus Christ, which requires full and complete acquiescence. The slothful person decides against letting Christ fully impact his or her life through the transformation promised by the risen Savior.

Dunnam and Reisman cite Henry Fairlie: "Sloth has been described in theology as 'hatred of all spiritual things which entail effort,' and 'fairheartedness in matters of difficulty,' in striving for perfection".[7] This thought informs this discourse because the Christian life of discipleship is built upon discipline, effort, and endurance. The process of sanctification (Paul's way of explaining the transformation God does through us after we give ourselves to following Jesus and His ways) requires effort, and the slothful person puts forth minimal effort and disregards the call to action from the Holy Spirit. Sloth undermines the work of God and is not congruent with holiness or the pursuit of it.

Effort and motivation define much of the spiritual journey we are all on individually and collectively. Without motivation, we never get started or sustain during challenging times. When we get knocked down, we have to be motivated to get back up. Without effort, we cannot follow through or ever achieve our purpose or finish a task. Can you think back to a time when something didn't go according to your plan? How did you handle it? Did you care? Did you do anything about it? When plans fail or change, motivation and effort are tools that are instrumental to any successes in this life.

When I was lying on the side of the road, I had the real thought that I can get up; I can shake this off. I'm okay. I'll just get up and stretch out my back…and find my shoulder bag…and my bike shoe…and MY BIKE, which was some 20 yards back down the road. I quickly realized I was not getting up as I labored to move. Then my thought changed: *if I just lie down, I'll be okay.* That didn't stop the pain either, and that is when I realized something was wrong and I needed help immediately.

Nehemiah was cupbearer to the king. He had a great position. He had authority and he only answered to the king of Babylonia. He knew that he had a good life and that he had it easy compared to other Jews and expatriates. He also knew that he could stay right where he was and never go back to Jerusalem or Israel and his life was going to be pretty good. But that was not what Nehemiah was going to do. He was cupbearer to the king, and now God was calling him right where he was to do what good needed doing right. Nehemiah needed to do something about his homeland.

You and I need to realize who we are in all aspects of life and where God's intervention is needed. For some of us, there is spiritual unrest; for others it's mental—our minds just aren't where they need to be. And for others, it is the physical realm that needs God's influence. To get healthier we must recognize who we are and who we want to become, but, more importantly, who God needs us to be.

Nehemiah realized he needed God's help right away. We see in Nehemiah 1:4, that he wept and mourned and fasted for days. There was fasting and weeping and much prayer. Nehemiah went to God immediately. From verse four through the rest of that chapter we see what Nehemiah prayed, what he went through, what was going on in his mind, and how he was asking for God's help.

He didn't just ask for help in restoring Israel. No, he prayed for forgiveness. He asked for God to forgive what his people had done, which had led to the exile. All of their lawlessness, their rejection of God's leadership, their worship of foreign gods and idols; he begged for God's forgiveness for all of that. He didn't argue that they should not have been exiled, or that they should not have been destroyed. He said, we deserved what you did, God. Please forgive us.

In our own lives, it can become so difficult to do this very thing. With our friends, neighbors, family, co-workers, or God, can we ask for forgiveness? Our ability to change course or recalibrate when we have made a mistake has a tremendous influence on our future.

One of the beauties of GPS navigation devices is it doesn't wait for us to decide if we should repent. Those systems don't ask us if we want to be forgiven. For most men, if we get lost…or *when* we get lost…or miss a turn, we try to figure it out on our own. This often results in us getting deeper into trouble and more lost. We get further off course. But, if we will listen, we will hear those familiar and comforting words: "Recalculating."

I love to run. I mean…I love to walk out the house in running shoes and shorts, and I like the freedom of putting one foot in front of the other…and running. I don't run with technology—no earbuds supplying a podcast, music, or a sermon to catch up on. It is my time to listen to God and clear my head. The problem is I am hard-headed, and I don't always know when to quit.

I went running in South Fulton County, GA one Friday afternoon in November. I was serving a church there, and it was an area I had not gotten to know yet. I started running, but I wasn't sure about where I was going. I knew this one road went north, but I thought it should turn east and start winding back south to bring me home. It was cool and was getting colder as the sun dropped in the sky.

Every bend in the road I neared, I *knew* was about to turn hard right to the east and start bringing me home. But every single bend straightened and did not turn toward home. I couldn't accept that I was running in the wrong direction. I…just…kept…running. Now, it was dark…like no moon in the sky dark, and I was lost in the cold. Well…I wasn't lost, so much as I was in the middle of the country, had been running for over an hour (~8 miles from home), and I didn't have the energy to turn around and run back home. That was when I realized I was in trouble.

As they say, *God looks out for children, drunks, and fools*. Not many cars passed by that night, but God was looking out for me. I nice, older man in a pickup truck stopped, and he asked if I needed help. God must have told him to help me, because I was shirtless and running in the dark in the middle of nowhere. I probably looked more like a threat than someone who needed help, but he stopped nonetheless and took me home.

While we may not always have a GPS to tell us how to get back on course, God is ever-ready to direct us there. When we are moving in the wrong direction, the answer is not to just keep going. Don't get me wrong; God doesn't call us to quit when tough times come, but God doesn't want us to persist when we are going in the opposite direction from Him.

Nehemiah did something really smart, something from which we should learn. Nehemiah begged for forgiveness because things had gotten so sideways between God and His people. With this realization, Nehemiah reminded God of His promises—he cited God's words to find redemption. In Nehemiah 1:9-10, he appealed to God's promise to Moses:

> "[B]ut *if* you return to Me and keep My command-
> ments and do them, though those of you who have
> been scattered were in the most remote part of the
> heavens, I will gather them from there and will
> bring them to the place where I have chosen to
> cause My name to dwell.' They are Your servants
> and Your people whom You redeemed by Your
> great power and by Your strong hand."

Nehemiah asked God to restore God's people. He knew that they were covenant people, and that meant something to God.

God had chosen the nation of Israel. He made a pact—a covenant—with them that He would be their God and they would be His people…forever. Nehemiah knew this, and he counted on it to get God moving in the direction of the Jews once more. He leveraged their status as God's chosen people and his status as the cupbearer to the king and asked God to get involved. Nehemiah asked for a second chance, and he promised God that they would do it right this time. And with everything he had in him, he would work to make it so.

For success in changing our ways, there also needs to be a realization that no matter how hard we try…no matter what we do… no matter who we think we can become, none of that matters. The most important influence on how we get healthier and rebuild ourselves is God. God is the only one who can move us to where we need to be. Unless we go to God and follow Nehemiah's example, we will never find the restoration we require. As Nehemiah said, "Lord, let your ear be attentive to the prayer of this your servant and to the prayer of your servants who delight in revering your name. Give your servant success today by granting him favor in the presence of this man" (Neh. 1:11ab, NIV). Knowing who we are often means being aware that we are in need. Like Nehemiah we must appeal to the One who made us and cares for us. God is the one who can heal all of our wounds. We must admit when we are lacking, and that scares us to death. But there must be a realization that we are missing the mark.

In the next chapter, we will look at taking the necessary steps to start rebuilding and getting healthier. But first, let us take a moment to follow Nehemiah's example. Join me in this prayer: Dear God, we have missed the mark. We have either made unhealthy decisions or choices for our lives or we have neglected what we knew to do, forgive us. Start again. Right now. Make Your Holy Spirit move in us this moment. Begin the rebuilding work. You never see us as lost causes, and may we never see ourselves or others that way. Today is a new day and the first of many of the road to health… and rebuilding our lives. Be with us, we pray in Jesus' name. Amen.

CHAPTER 2

KNOW WHAT YOU ARE GETTING INTO

NEHEMIAH KNEW EXACTLY WHAT he was dealing with: his homeland was in ruins. Animals roamed the countryside, moving their way through Jerusalem. Drifters moved just as easily through their land. Think of destruction in your mind. Think about England after the countless bombing runs of the German Lufstopa designed to bring a nation to surrender. Or try envisioning the pictures from the great San Francisco earthquake in 1906 or the pictures of years and years of civil war in Lebanon—shocking a once beautiful nation into rubble and destruction.

That is what happened to Judah, and specifically Jerusalem. It was a hot mess. There was no valid leadership; only corrupted landlords who wanted to maintain their control. The people had no identity or comprehension of their covenant with God, and even if they had, they didn't know where to begin to reconcile their relationship with God. Nehemiah knew this. He had news from the boots (or sandals) on the ground. They needed help quickly, and Nehemiah was ready to act.

Nehemiah needed to return to Jerusalem on a temporary basis. He had a limited amount of time to get the work done. These

bodies we have are on loan from God until one day, they are perfected in eternity, returning to what God intended for us. These
bodies are not ours. God has given them to us to serve God. With
all that we have we are to serve God. Holistically, we are all connected, just as the different aspects of ourselves are connected.

As a Wesleyan—a practitioner of the theology and understanding of John Wesley, the 18th Century Anglican priest and
founder of Methodism—I know what holism looks like. There is
a connection between the body, mind, and the soul. Wesley sought
to make his parishioners healthier by understanding how much
control they had on their physical health, which is often a reflection
of spiritual health. I say *often* to acknowledge the people who deal
with disabilities and physical limitations that they do not merit nor
deserve. I contend that if we live to excess in any one area of our
lives, that imbalance will manifest in our spiritual journey as well.

Wesley was not one to shy away from topics that may not have
seemed like the normal discussion for Anglican priests, and the
world still benefits from his courage. In the Foreword of *Primitive
Physick*, Francis Asbury and Thomas Coke support Wesley's
approach to health and explain to fellow Methodists in America
that while they are concerned with the souls of the people called
Methodists, they are concerned with their bodies as well.[8] Holism
was instrumental to the beginning of the Methodist movement
in America, which by the early 20th Century had grown to be the
largest Protestant denomination in the country. Holism firmly
anchored Wesley's approach to life and his hopes for other disciples of Jesus.

Randy L. Maddox cites Wesley and his views of natural remedies and ways to live a healthy lifestyle from *Primitive Physick*.
He promoted physical health not for the sake of wellness alone,

but his motivation was for eternal restoration and in support of a holistic approach to salvation and wellness: "Yet (like the early Greek theologians) Wesley insisted throughout his life that salvation must involve not only inner holiness but also the recovery of actual moral righteousness in our outward lives".[9] Wesley champions the holistic view of health and commends the love of God as the ultimate remedy: "And by the unspeakable joy, and perfect calm, serenity, and tranquility it gives the mind, it becomes the most powerful of all means of health and long life."[10] Wesley advocates an all-encompassing Christian way of life rooted in his understanding that God does not want illness of soul or mind or body for humanity.

In *Primitive Physick*, Wesley's Preface includes the statement, "The entire creation was at peace with man, so long as man was at peace with his Creator."[11] Maddox expands on Wesley's statement to declare that disease and illness are the result of sin and the Fall.[12] He believes Wesley had "a strong emphasis on the importance of hygiene, diet, and exercise for recovering or maintaining health."[13] Wesley commends a proper diet as an exercise in thoughtful planning and logic: "Yet steadily observe both that kind and measure of food, which experience shews to be most friendly to strength and health."[14] God is longing to heal humanity's spiritual disease of sin, and while advocating that point and incorporating it into his systematic theology—his full understanding of and belief in God— Wesley emphasizes holistic health, including diet and exercise.

Wesley gives clear direction on what to eat and drink and when to sleep in *Primitive Physick*. He also does not neglect to instruct on the subject of exercise: "The power of exercise, both to preserve and restore health, is greater than can well be conceived."[15] He even advises where to exercise: "Use as much exercise daily in open air, as you can without weariness."[16] Wesley touted exercise as necessary to a long and healthy life and as an asset to overcoming weakness: "We may strengthen any weak part of the body by constant exercise."[17] He does not commend exercise as isolated focus but as part of a holistic pursuit of life. Just as people should not solely commit themselves to exercise, neither should scholars direct their efforts merely to the study of books: "The studious ought to have stated times for exercise, at least two or three hours a-day: the one half of this before dinner, the other before going to bed."[18] Wesley promotes a balanced approach to life and health.

What is truly amazing to me about John Wesley is the guy wrote about this stuff in the 18th Century. He actually looked at the world around him and made some observations and suggestions, hoping to improve it. If our mindset was the same as some of those great church leaders, many of the ills of society would be addressed in the name and power of Jesus. Jesus came to change lives, and our refusal to embrace the transformation that comes with following Jesus negates the grace He so freely offers.

In our contemporary world, there are leaders who are unafraid to proclaim the Good News. I am a huge fan of the rap artist Lecrae. Lecrae is a follower of Jesus, and, by all accounts, he lives his faith and keeps it at the center of his music career. In 2017, Lecrae declared that it was time for his faith to be a more central part of his music and ministry. Lecrae declared his separation from the white evangelical church in an interview on the show, "Truth Talk."

Lecrae has spoken at the Catalyst Conference and has appeared at other popular Christian events that are heavily white evangelical. But Lecrae has felt the need to announce his separation from white evangelicalism, and it began because of the reaction he had to the Michael Brown shooting. Michael Brown was shot and killed by

St. Louis police officers for refusing to obey police officers and advancing on them. He was unarmed. This tragic event shook the nation and led to further division.

Lecrae spoke about his outrage and people inside his sphere of influence—many being white evangelicals—lashed out against him. Lecrae describes how he processed this disconnect: "The visceral attacks that came my way were like a shock to my system. That did some identity work."[19] Lecrae shared a view he believed is grounded in the Gospel, but he believed white evangelicals were choosing to make the *white* more important than the *evangelical* part of their identity.

This is a not a form of identity theology, where faith is divided up based on which group you identify with best. The Gospel is larger than race or culture, and that truth needed to be avowed to declare that evangelicalism is bigger than race. In the same way, pastors have to be better at attacking issues of the day without regard for the popularity of the stance or the offense that may follow. If someone is trapped in a house that is on fire, you don't waste time trying to save the flower bed...you break down the door and get the people out. If followers of Jesus are obese or sedentary or addicted to food or other substances, you don't preach more about salvation; you preach about addressing those sins in the process of living out that salvation.

How often do we have preachers today who talk about this topic? How often do we hear secular leaders encouraging exercise and nutrition? We like to talk about healthcare costs, but we don't want to talk about prevention. We'd rather pay for treatment and medical solutions to our problems after we have done significant damage to ourselves. Maybe we should focus less on passing laws to take away the tough choices and emphasize the benefits and results of smart, healthy choices.

You may wonder where are those voices. I don't know. I have felt so convicted along these lines, which is why I wrote this book. I truly believe this refusal to connect our faith with how we live our lives (including what we put into our bodies and how we use them) is the number one issue destroying the church. Leaders need to take more accountability for ourselves.

Jesus tells a parable about readiness in Luke 12, and people take away different meanings from that parable. Jesus is teaching about being prepared. He tells a story about a master who goes out of town for a wedding. His servants don't know when he is going to return, and they have a choice to make: they can either live it up, ignoring their tasks and letting the estate come into dis-repair or they can work like the master is returning at any moment. Peter—one of Jesus' closest friends and disciples, himself, is con-fused about whom Jesus is talking.

Jesus explains that a good servant—a steward of what his master has given him—works hard while his master is away without knowing when the master will return. Bad servants eat, drink, and are merry while the master is gone, pretending the master will never return only to be punished when he does return. Jesus sums up His intent with one verse: "From everyone who has been given much, much will be required; and to whom they entrusted much, of him they will ask all the more" (Luke 12:48b, NASB). This is a lesson not just for Peter, but for all of us who are leaders…and servants.

I have two children: Hannah and Joseph. We moved to Valdosta, GA because God called us to start a church, and we didn't know a soul there. This type of church plant model is referred to as a parachute drop, and from first-hand experience, it is not for the faint of heart. It did feel, at times, like we were dropped into a war-zone, and all four of us were receiving enemy fire. It was a lonely time, and we tried to find some friends.

One place we found friends was other pastor families. During our first dinner at a brand new friend's house, we were having a lovely time. Joseph was five years old, and he has always been a bit of a migrating diner—he eats better on the move. This can be quite annoying for his parents, but if it helps him eat, we live with it. This night, he got up from the table and was playing with the other children who were done with dinner. The parents continued on with our happy evening, and then we heard a solid thump on the hardwood floor of the home. I hate that sound…I have heard it before! I knew what that particular sound meant, and we had to spring into action.

Joseph was still facedown on the floor when we got to him, and I saw blood and what looked like a tooth, double the normal size. We scooped him up, and all I could think as I held one of his two front teeth in my hand was, Oh, no! This is a baby tooth but it came out with the root! He will never have a normal smile. He's five, and this moment on these slick, and ridiculously hard, hard-wood-floors has changed his life.

Joseph slipped and fell face-first so fast that he was unable to get his hands up in time. One of those front teeth was knocked out, and the other was knocked crooked. He cried as I held him. Joseph has always had a high pain tolerance because of some other issues he has dealt with his whole life, so I knew he was more scared than hurt. The four genius adults in the room didn't know what to do about the now dislodged tooth and root. The consensus was—left to our own intellect and a registered nurse who shall remain nameless—was to put the tooth back into place. Yikes! That was as miserable as you would think it would be for Joseph and for his parents.

This was a job for Daddy, so my wife, Lindsey, held him while I washed the tooth and then tried to return it to its home. I pushed; my amazing son tolerated it and squirmed a little. I pushed some more, and he took it. When I got done, it looked right, but things were now askew. I called the dentist from the town we had moved from, because we didn't even have one in our new city yet. He said, in no uncertain terms, DO NOT put the tooth back in; it will cause an infection. Next, I got the great honor of removing the tooth from its original home after it had settled back in place. That was fun! And, yes, Joseph does still love me, but he does keep his distance from time to time with a noticeable tick when I mention teeth or if I act like I know how to care for any medical issues. Truth be told, after the tooth was removed for the second time, he went back to playing once the bleeding stopped, and he even ate some, too.

We saw a problem, and we had no idea how to fix it. It was not a mistake to love him during his time of need, but he needed more than we had to offer. So many people are dealing with an unhealthy lifestyle, either because of bad food choices, the inability to control the amount they eat, or a lack of physical activity. It usually comes on slowly, but the acute stage of *unhealth* arrives eventually. We are certainly supposed to love people at all times, but they need more than that to get the help they need.

Trying the self-help approach is admirable, but jumping on the newest and latest fad diet or buying the trendiest piece of workout equipment usually results in relapses and new coatracks in our bedrooms and family rooms, oddly resembling treadmills and ellipticals. It is like me trying to ram that tooth back into my son's head. Sure, we are doing something that feels constructive, but, in the grand scheme of things, we are only hurting ourselves by making the problem worse.

We will not be able to address the problems around our health without God. It is God who created us, and it is God who can restore us. If we can engage God and lean on His strength, we will be able to fight the growing epidemic of poor and unsustainable health.

As a pastor and leader in my community, I am haunted by God's words to His prophet Ezekiel. God calls Ezekiel to be His prophet and gives him a message to deliver to God's people, who once again have turned away from God and what God wants for them, in rebellion to God's authority and leadership. (This, of course, is a familiar situation we find ourselves in as Americans AND as the church.) In Ezekiel 3, God, having called the prophet, now commissions him with a final message. God says, you will speak My words to the wicked and to the righteous that fall away. But, if you do not warn them of the disaster that is to befall them, "his blood I will require at your hand" (Ezek. 3:18c, NASB).

Men and women—religious and secular authorities alike— have been positioned to shepherd the people. If we do not warn those in harm's way of the pending disaster and if we do not assist our brothers and sisters in their times of need, we will bear the blame. Yes, they are accountable to God for their actions (or lack of healthy lifestyles), but we will be accountable as well. That truth haunts me!

So, why is it, you ask, that there is such silence or lack of conviction from leaders about health and wellness. It is puzzling in light of God's direction in the Bible. One reason we don't hear enough from leadership is because so many leaders don't want to live up to the standards we know are right. If a preacher prays frequently in his or her personal life, he or she will talk about praying because it comes easier to them. They obviously believe in God's direction to do it because they use part of their valuable time to do it. If a politician cares about the environment, they will pass laws to make people drive a hybrid car or truck or force companies to invest in solar energy.

If a preacher sees people on a daily basis as part of the church he serves who are unhealthy—worse or the same as he or she is—why would they point it out? It is embarrassing and challenging to admit you have a problem and talk about an aspect of life that needs drastic improvement. This occurs in the same way a politician preaches about conservation while living in an enormous house with a significant environmental footprint. We don't want to have to change ourselves, our behavior or change our comfort level.

A second reason leaders in authority don't address uncomfortable topics is we want to make people happy. This is a particular disorder for many pastors. We don't want to tell people, no! No, you should probably never go to an all-you-can-eat buffet because no one should ever eat *all they can eat* at one sitting. (This is a standing rule for me as I have a tendency to overeat in the pursuit to *get my money's worth*.) No, the 2-3 hours Wesley recommends in the pursuit of recreation were not to be spent on the couch watching television shows or playing video games. No, you shouldn't choose watching sports over your family in the pursuit of fulfillment. One group knows who you are and loves you anyway, and the other will never know your name but covets your money and your time.

Who wakes up each morning, desiring to be the *heavy* who has to tell people, no? Well…it doesn't matter if we *want* to say those words to others or ourselves. Leadership of a church, a business, or a household is not about popularity. Whether we are considering the gift of life, a spouse, children, or a corporation, they are all significant. Leaders who only say what is popular are usually forgotten once they move on, once their target audience moves on to the next shiny toy or flittering butterfly that draws their attention, or when they die.

Some of the kings of Israel and Judah probably wish they were forgotten, because, to quote Babu Bhatt from "Seinfeld" fame: Each was a "very bad man! Very, very bad!" King Ahaz ruled Judah, and he was *very, very bad*. He worshipped other gods. He closed the temple of God. He went to other nations for help, and not God. When he died, they did not bury him with the kings of Jerusalem to verify his low status as a king.

King Hezekiah, his son, followed him and ruled Judah from 715–687 B.C. There was a big difference between them: "He did right in the sight of the LORD, according to all that his father David had done" (2 Chron. 29:2, NASB). Hezekiah realized the nation had fallen very far away from God's plan, and they were not keeping their end of the covenant with God. In his first month as king—no need to waste time *getting back right*—he called in the priests to consecrate themselves, wipe out the worship of other gods, and get the Temple open and operating. God's prophets—Nathan, Gad, and David—gave Hezekiah direction, and he did what God wanted him to do.

The author of 2 Chronicles details all that King Hezekiah did and explains how he lived his life: "[H]e did what was good, right and true before the LORD his God" (2 Chron. 31:20b, NASB). He served and lived in stark contrast to his father, Ahaz, and God was watching…and so were his people. When Hezekiah died, he was buried in the upper section of the tombs of the kings, and he was honored by all of the people of Jerusalem and Judah (2 Chron. 32:33, NASB).

Leaders who deliver a message because it is *good, right and true* leave a legacy that outlives them and the people they initially spoke to and helped. Those are the people we want to be. Much as John Wesley is still talked about over 225 years after his death, we want to leave that legacy. No matter what our kingdom looks like—a home, a neighborhood, an office, a community, our own life—it should be dedicated to God and God's purposes.

We need to remind ourselves of Jesus' words, "From everyone who has been given, much will be required; and to whom they entrusted much, of him they will ask all the more." We have been given much. As Ezekiel was charged in his commissioning, if he didn't deliver God's saving words to His people, their "blood I will require at your hand." These are sobering messages, and truths we know apply to us as leaders. And I know some of you are reading this and thinking, I'm not a leader. But you are. You are your brother's or your sister's keeper. Yes, you! You can influence the world around you. If you are a follower of Jesus, you are bound to serve and care, leading others to the best image of themselves. If you aren't a follower, you have the potential to be, and that means you can go ahead and act like you are and care about others. God loves us all, and He wants ALL of us to follow Jesus.

God has given us minds and intellects that explore the galaxy. We have been blessed with bodies that we can push beyond our perceived limitations. Inside of us, we have been entrusted with souls that are immortal. We are gifted beyond measure, and God is calling us to be healthier.

God is able to heal bodies, minds and souls, and means are available to humanity that will contribute to health and wellness. Wesley saw exercise, diet, and spirituality as important factors to overall health. After emphasizing these factors and the importance of rest, he added, "Above all, add to the rest, (for it is no labour lost) that old unfashionable medicine, prayer."[20] Holism is a valuable motivation for a life dedicated to holiness in the Wesleyan way.

Theologian Gregory S. Clapper agrees that Wesley's understanding of the Christian life is holistic in nature and design. Clapper describes Wesley's approach as threefold: orthodoxy, orthopraxis, and orthokardia. The right beliefs, right action, and right heart are the keys to holiness and life as a disciple of Jesus (Collins and Tyson 216). Clapper expands, "When the Christian way of life (described not by only one or two, but all three of the *orthos*) is embodied in real-life believers, it is itself the best proclamation of the gospel possible" (219). The purpose for individuals is not solely to witness about their faith, but the pursuit of holiness is a sufficient and necessary witness.

Whenever I think about *praxis*, I am reminded of Allen Iverson. Iverson is an NBA Hall of Fame point guard and shooting guard who played for 14 seasons. He was known to be a tough player who never gave into injuries and scored at will, no matter how many shots it took or falls to the court were required. A very famous dustup happened between Iverson and his Hall of Fame head coach, Larry Brown.

Iverson was criticized by his coach for skipping or not working hard in practice as Brown desired more effort and leadership from Iverson in workouts. Iverson famously responded, "I's supposed to be the franchise player, and we in here talking about practice. Mean, listen; we talking about practice. Not a game. Not a game. Not a game. But practice." The preparation was not as important to Iverson, because he felt like he was giving it all when it counted. He thought he was doing enough.

Many of us feel like we are doing enough. We feel like our hearts are right, or we may feel like my understanding is right. One or two of the *orthos* is not enough. *We talking about praxis.* The Christian walk of faith requires *right action* as well as belief and commitment. So, yes, we talking about *praxis.*

Wesley scholar Randy L. Maddox describes further how Wesley saw health and physical wellness as part of faith and holiness. Wesley suggests that Christians cannot simply indulge every urge and want they have. That life is not only unhealthy, but that manner of living is not congruent with Scripture or Christian history: "'[S]elf denial' is indispensible to the Christian life. One practice on which he laid particular emphasis (due to assumed primitive precedent) was regular fasting."[21] Wesley recognized the benefit of allowing room for God by offering God control of the body: "Nothing conduces more to health, than abstinence and plain food, with due labour."[22] Wesley's views on wellness and the emphasis he placed on healthy living shows that Christians certainly have tools available to them that contribute to holiness.

It takes a great deal of effort to achieve real health for the body, mind, and soul, but we can do it with God's help. As the great theologian from "Pale Rider" teaches us, we need to drag our bodies into the fight. Clint Eastwood plays a preacher who comes as an answer to a young woman's prayer for a miracle. As Eastwood comes to the aid of a group of prospectors, they need loads of help.

A large boulder is impeding the creek they are panning for gold. One of their leaders tries to dissuade Preacher from taking part in the sledgehammering of the boulder. Eastwood's character says, "The spirit ain't worth spit without a little exercise." They get after that boulder, and they finally remove it. There is enough work for all of us to get done.

Unlike others who may push the fasting and abstinence ideals to the extreme, nearly resembling self-mutilation and masochism, Wesley was not interested in such things. Wesley saw this practice of self-denial as a way to give something to God, not take away from the human life: "For Wesley, self-denial had nothing to do with physical abuse of oneself, but was rather a willingness to embrace God's will when it is contrary to one's own."[23] Charles Yrigoyen, Jr. states that Wesley avowed fasting as biblically based and included abstinence from food as well as limited eating and drinking. He details three of Wesley reasons for fasting: sorrow for sin, penitence for overeating or excessive drinking, and enrichment of one's prayer life.[24]

Intermittent Fasting (I.F.) has become very popular these days. I.F. is the practice of reduced food consumption for intermittent periods throughout the day. That means practitioners may not eat breakfast or lunch, but they do eat dinner. People pick a small window of the day to consume food. They may decide to eat only during a two-hour or four-hour window each day. The proponents suggest that this approach kick-starts the metabolism and makes your body more efficient at burning energy.

Wesley's message is not just for those in the Wesleyan way but for all of those who desire to be healthier. These means of self-denial can also be a part of Wesley's works of mercy (caring for those in need) where regular abstinence from food can provide one with money that can be used for feeding others and serving God's purposes. Physical health does not benefit just the individual but also those who are served.

Nehemiah's effort to rebuild his home was not just for him; it was for his nation and his progeny. Nehemiah had work to do, and the clock was ticking. He went to the king with a mission and a plan: to get permission to lead the effort to rebuild Jerusalem and to go with the king's blessing.

Nehemiah knew it was going to take a bold endeavor, but he first had to get the king on his side. Nehemiah goes to King Artaxerxes and assumes his normal position. Wine is to be served. Nehemiah says he was not normally EVER sad in the presence of the king, but that day was different (Neh. 2:1, NASB). And he was scared—unbelievably scared. We see the exchange in Nehemiah 2:2, "So the king said to me, 'Why is your face sad though you are not sick? This is nothing but sadness of heart.' Then I was very much afraid." (Even King Artaxerxes knows that the body and spirit are connected—"sadness of heart.") Nehemiah has his chance.

Like a band aid being ripped off a barely healed cut, the skin needs to be pulled all at once to avoid tearing the skin slowly, prolonging the agony. Nehemiah dove in: "I said to the king, 'Let the king live forever. Why should my face not be sad when the city, the place of my fathers' tombs, lies desolate and its gates have been consumed by fire?'" (Neh. 2:3, NASB). No getting that horse back in the barn! The ball was rolling for sure now.

Artaxerxes asks why Nehemiah looks so glum. At first, we think, the king must really care for him. But let's be realistic: Nehemiah is the sommelier for the king, which means he tastes all of the wine for vintage as well as safety. Nehemiah just gave the king a cup of wine. Artaxerses is concerned about himself…as most of us would be with assassins on the loose…and he is the ruler of the greatest empire of the day. He is a little nervous when he sees *his* wine taster looking pinked.

So, he asks why Nehemiah looks so awful, or as Peterson says in *The Message*, "hangdog." He must have looked pretty bad for the king to have even noticed, but it was, after all, in his own self-interest, a smart thing to do. God uses this moment of doubt & ego-centricity to open the door just enough.

Artaxerxes is so relieved Nehemiah has not given him tainted wine, Nehemiah probably could have asked for part of the kingdom. Artaxerxes nearly lets out an audible swoosh. "What do you need?! I'll give you whatever you want!" Nehemiah swallows hard…takes a quick second, which probably felt like an hour, and swung for the fences. No request is too bold when God is doing the directing. When the One who spoke the world into being says, "Move," you move. "I need to go home!"

Why should I not be upset? he asks rhetorically. "Something is wrong…drastically wrong, if you want to know the whole truth. And I have to do something about it." Nehemiah says, "My family's graves have been destroyed and desecrated—destroyed and have been irrevocably damaged. The city of our God is destroyed, without a gate or walls. We have no means to return to normalcy, to reintroduce our culture, or establish a basic standard of living." Nehemiah was heartbroken.

The king wanted to know one thing: "What would you request?" (Neh. 2:4a, NASB) "Don't beat around the bush," as my wife says. What can I do to help you out? What is it going to take? Nehemiah takes a breath, prays to God, which we cannot discount or ignore, and makes a bold request: help me rebuild my homeland (Neh. 2:5, NASB). Please don't miss how bold this is. This is the homeland of the king's former enemies. He didn't ask to go back to start a business or develop a charity network to care for the poor. No, Nehemiah said, let me go back to rebuild my city and eventually our nation.

King Artaxerxes is unfazed by the request (this is where Nehemiah's prayer has such a tremendous impact), and he wants to do a little house cleaning and find out the details, such as the length of travel and the duration of the project (6a, NASB). Nehemiah prayed, and God intervened. There is no reason Artaxerxes should have helped Nehemiah and these former enemies. I would think that many of his fellow countrymen and women would have expected the king to continue to oppress and reign over this nation so much blood and treasure had been spent to defeat. But, God is able to change people's minds, and God is able to do exceedingly more than we can even conceive. The pump was primed with prayer, and God's plan was set in motion.

When we are damaged on the outside, in our minds, or in our souls, we have to get to the point where we say, "Why should I not be upset with where I am right now?! Why would I not want to get help?! Why would I not want to make myself better?!" That is when we begin to think, I need to get moving on this plan to reconcile things or to make things better than they are.

As I was lying on the gurney in the trauma unit of Georgia Regents University Medical Center (the old Medical College of Georgia Hospital), the appraisal began: examinations and x-rays and scans. My wife and a close friend of ours were there with me after they made the drive to Augusta. The reports and diagnoses started coming in with a laundry list of injuries and fractures: the first issue, and the most painful for me, was my back.

They initially said I had a broken pelvis and sacrum, then that was changed to *just* severely bruised. Next, I was told I fractured the L1 vertebra, described as a compression fracture. This injury to my spine was also connected to the compression of my lower back, which was severely bruised. Those injuries were eventually fully realized over a year later. At that time I was on to my third opinion from another orthopedic practice for help with my back, and that doctor described the lower part of my spine as a "big, bony mess." (The compressed spine injury, which doesn't un-compress by the way, is why years later I still cannot sit without discomfort.) I also was diagnosed with a concussion, bruised ribs, fractured tibia, fractured fibula in two places, fractured talus bone, broken toe, lacerated leg, lacerated tongue, chipped tooth; and road rash to round out the damage from the accident.

After hearing all of the different things that were wrong with me, it was then that I began to get an idea of just what this recovery was going to take. This would have been the time for fears and the thoughts of what ifs (lost ability, inability, limited recovery, brain damage,…) to overpower me and my family. But I had such a tangible experience of God's peace throughout this trauma from the moment it happened, even to the point of the physical assessment.

To give you a full understanding of me and how my mind works, it was at this moment when I decided to talk with the Head of the Trauma Unit at GRU. (This man had decades of experience in trauma units, and I knew he would be able to give me a real assessment.) "I am supposed to run the 2014 Boston Marathon in April (the accident was July 17, 2013), do you think I can still run?" I will never forget his response. He looked me up and down as I laid there, mangled and bleeding, and said, "Probably." *So, you're telling me there's a chance.* I continued to ask that question of my varying healthcare professionals throughout this process, and nobody ever told me, no. That was good enough for me.

I qualified for the Boston Marathon in November 2012 at the Rock'n'Roll Savannah Marathon. The bombings happened just a few months later as the entire running world stopped to pause and assess what had actually happened. Then, I resolved to never forget the victims and to never cower to cowards who attacked innocents and our way of life. I was bound and determined to run in the first marathon following the killings as a show of solidarity with the victims and with Boston. (My mom is an alumna of Boston University and a Rhode Islander. So, even though I am from Georgia, I have always had a strong connection to New England.)

For someone who was still strapped to a gurney, the question for the trauma chief was a bold, if not insane, request. I asked him if I could run the race in April, and he never said no. He did the math, and speculated I MIGHT be able to run again in 5-6 months. Of course, that meant surgery to repair my leg, which would have to wait for two weeks for the swelling to go down, and four more weeks on my back to heal the spinal fracture and learning to walk again and then run and countless hours of physical therapy to help me do those things. I had a long road ahead of me to say the very least.

Artaxerses says, "How long will you be gone?" How Nehemiah's heart must have burned inside of his chest in that moment. It was music to his ears. Without really understanding what he was getting into, Nehemiah thanked God and spit out a timeframe with no knowledge of how credible it was. God told Noah to build a boat big enough for two of every animal. God sent Abraham to a foreign land. God told Moses to take on the superpower of his day and lead a nation into the wilderness for 40 years. God told a shepherd boy to take on a giant. Now God was telling a royal sommelier to become a contractor and leader of men and women. All Nehemiah had ever done was follow and serve a king, now he was serving the one King, God the Creator and Master Builder.

God intervenes and gives Nehemiah a timeframe. Artaxerses looks over at his wife, the queen, who nods approval. The king gives him permission to go. Most of us would have stopped here. Most of us would have backed out of the king's presence as fast as we could curtsey and backstep. Not Nehemiah…no…Nehemiah swings for the fences. God says ask for what you will need RIGHT NOW! Do not wait until later. Be bold. Ask right now.

Nehemiah had a plan to rebuild. He asked the king for letters to the governors of the regions he would be passing through to give him safe passage to Judah and a letter for the royal forester for a big request (Neh. 2:7-8, NASB). Nehemiah was very bold! He asked for the timber to build the gates of a fortress, the walls of the city, and a home for him to live in while he did the work. King Artaxerxes did exactly what Nehemiah asked of him. The winebearer made (with God's help) the king of the most powerful kingdom around do exactly what he needed him to do. Thanks be to God!!!

Nehemiah was bold. Again and again, he made big asks and large demands for the sole purpose of fulfilling God's vision. We, too, should be bold when it comes to getting healthier, but at the same time we do not want to be unrealistic in our expectations. There is a delicate balance, but boldness is not something we should lack because God honors that.

If you need to lose a hundred pounds, be bold: set that goal and work toward it. But we must be realistic. As the saying goes, Rome wasn't built in a day. Conversely, the Roman Empire wasn't destroyed in a day either. There were many bad decisions that led to the fall of the greatest empire of the day, whose greatness is seen in its influence on the modern world. Many of us have made bad decision after bad decision. Our imbalance in our bodies, minds, or souls didn't happen over night, but none of us is too far gone to make a change. We can look at *rebuilding* Rome, and it certainly will take longer than a day or two.

Nehemiah knew what he was getting into, and he didn't make the decision to do something lightly. The tension was written all over his face, and his heart was aching inside of his chest. This was going to be an amazing story of redemption and restoration, and Nehemiah had a huge part to play. Now, it was time to do something.

It was famously said by President Theodore Rosevelt, "Walk softly and carry a big stick." While this sounds like a great plan for a hunting trip, it also seems like a great way to carry out God's plans. Except for Nehemiah, it was more like, "Walk softly and carry letters from the king of the world *and* walk with part of his army *with* horses and chariots." People have a tendency to get out of your way, and they did the same for Nehemiah. The leaders of the resistance to his plans learned about what he wanted to do, and they did nothing. They were *displeased*, but that was all they were, because Nehemiah was walking with a big *army* and because God was with him.

Nehemiah asks for a passport stamped by King Artaxerses himself. Check. You know Asaph, the master lumberjack…the big brawny guy with the flannel robe & big biceps…can you send him a requisition order for the lumber I will need to build the temple and the wall around the city, AND for a house that I will build in which to live? Sure. Why not?! Artaxerses says, "I'll throw in a cavalry and letters to protect you against any enemy that even thinks about stopping you."

A cynic might suggest that Nehemiah had given the king some heavy pours to prime the pump. Maybe he waited until Artaxerses was good and lubricated, primed for a big request. Sure, that makes sense, but we already saw the answer earlier in Nehemiah's story: he fasted and prayed…for God and God's purposes. That is the only way Artaxerses would ever have agreed to do what he did that day.

Nehemiah asked him for a trip to the moon and back. The king will have to trust in a new sommelier. He is giving tons of timber away for nothing. It was a big, lucrative, blank check. Nehemiah is sent out as a conquering hero. Just like his ancestors when God conquered another superpower of their day in Egypt, Nehemiah left with the spoils he needed. The first of God's miracles to help rebuild Jerusalem had occurred, and now Nehemiah had to respond in kind to God's faithfulness.

In the next chapter, we will look at what it takes to rebuild and be restored.

CHAPTER 3

THE WAY TO GETTING BETTER

WHAT DOES IT TAKE for transformation? It takes God. It requires our reliance and dependence on God. For Nehemiah, it took God's hand helping him, "And the king granted them to me because the good hand of God was on me" (Neh. 2:8b, NASB). Nehemiah knew what he was getting into, and he knew he needed God to take care of it. With God's guidance, Nehemiah was able to move forward with God's plan. Of course, now the hard part would begin: How do you rebuild a nation?

> "Then I came to the governors *of the provinces* beyond the River and gave them the king's letters. Now the king had sent with me officers of the army and horsemen. When Sanballat the Horonite and Tobiah the Ammonite official heard *about it*, it was very displeasing to them that someone had come to seek the welfare of the sons of Israel." (Neh. 2:9-10, NASB)

It did not take long before resistance happened. The leaders back home in Judah were ready to steal Nehemiah's sunshine as soon as they heard about his plans. One after the other, as

Nehemiah met the governors of the regions west of the Euphrates, he showed them his passport—his *Get Out of Jail Free* card. He kept moving west, but he was moving slowly with all that timber, so the governors smiled as they read his authorization and sent word to their fellow governors in Judah to start making a plan. And they did.

They sent messengers that easily outpaced Nehemiah and his entourage. They went straight to Sanballat and Tobiah—the governors of Judea. They were outraged, not because someone wanted to spruce the place up, but because someone was coming who had something they did not: real concern for God's people. Sanballat and Tobiah were politicians; they did everything they could to stay in power. They wanted to keep the Jewish people down. They wanted them divided on issues. They wanted them to maintain their defeated mindset. Those two wanted the people to continue as lost sheep in the wilderness with no shepherd to lead them. But…Nehemiah—God's chosen one—was coming.

Sanballat and Tobiah did not live in Jerusalem. They did not need to live there. They were safer outside the city in fortresses of their own. They missed Nehemiah's arrival…they had to have missed it. Nehemiah shows up with ton after ton of lumber and a royal cavalry, and a full caravan of servants and travelers. He found a place to get situated, and he waited. I would imagine it was quite a ruckus, but God made sure no one noticed. Well…at least if they did, they did not get bothered by what they saw.

Not wanting to seem too anxious, Nehemiah waited three days. He prayed. He waited. For all we know, Sanballat and Tobiah were away on a trip, inspecting sections of the province they governed. Nehemiah rested and prepared himself for what God had for him to do. He told no one what his mission was. Quietly and casually,

Nehemiah got up in the middle of the night, and he went to inspect the wall. He rode his donkey and a few men walked with him.

Section by section, Nehemiah tried to get his mind around what needed to be done. He passed the Valley Gate. He moved to the Dragon's Fountain and to the Refuse Gate, which is a horrible name for a gate and certainly paints a picture. He moved to the Fountain gate and then to the king's pool, but the rubble was so bad that Nehemiah could not reach it on his donkey. He moved through the valley, around the debris and barriers, making his way to the Valley Gate. He did all of this in the cover of night, unnoticed by the officials and the residents. All of this had a purpose.

Nehemiah had to know how bad it was for himself. He could not rely on someone else to tell him what they thought of the disaster or his plan to build again. He would not let anyone start constructing a wall of opposition to what God called him to build. He did not tell the Jewish leaders who wanted the same things he did nor the ones who might oppose him. Nehemiah did not tell the people he would need to help lead the people or the actual workforce to get the job done. He simply got an in-depth view of the state of things, and things were as bad as he had been told they were. Now, it was time for the plan to begin.

There needs to be a plan. There must be a procedure or course of action to address the malady or brokenness. When people have come to me asking about what to do to get into running, I offer them a plan. I say, begin by running until you can't run anymore, or pretend like someone is chasing you. If you can't pretend, then get someone to chase you. I have heard that dumping a cup of ice water on someone does the trick. That is NOT actually what I say. I suggest the Couch to 5k program.

I believe in that program because it forces one to realize I am on a couch, and I must get off the couch and do something different from what I have been doing. It balances walking and running with different time intervals for each to help build endurance. (The program doesn't really allow for any more couch time, so you do that on your own.) I have also developed a program called *Exerceo Divina* to improve people's health. My program was developed during my doctoral research to find a means for holistic health. My program showed a statistically significant improvement in health (lowered blood pressure) after utilizing *Exerceo Divina*, which will be covered later and is listed in the appendices.[25]

Any time we try to rebuild ourselves or even just make some self-improvements, there will be resistance. Sometimes that resistance will come from within or from others close to us. Sometimes it comes from people we don't even know who are jealous of what we are trying to do and they see the successes we are having. But we are just like Nehemiah: they cannot stop us from beginning our good work. They can stand there and point their fingers or wag their tongues at us, but that is all they are able to do…that is all God allows them to do. We are walking with a big army as well. While they may be an invisible, divine army, they are with us to face any foe. Others may be displeased, but they cannot do anything to us or to ruin our good work.

Wall builders have to know where their strengths are, and that is who you and I are—wall builders. For us to rebuild ourselves, we need to understand what our *army* is—what are our abilities and the weapons needed to repair and get back to wholeness. We do not instinctually know how strong we are, because the world is so good at telling us we aren't good enough or we are lacking in one way or another. To understand our strengths, we need to get perspective on the way that God created us and what are our inherent abilities.

Human beings are not made up of one substance. While we are precious to God, we are not diamonds—valuable rocks that are perfect, strong, and beautiful, but that is all they are. (Well, except my daughter, she is precious and perfect and beautiful.) But human beings are made up of more than just one substance. There is more to us than meets the eye…literally.

My brother-in-law received his undergraduate degree from Emory University. He was able to participate in a research project on the eye while he was there. His article was titled, "Pharmacokinetics of Intraocular Drug Delivery by Periocular Injections Using Ocular Fluorophotometry."[26] I don't know what a lot of those words mean, but they were able to reach some conclusions about "how to treat rear eye diseases through injections and testing how permeable the sclera (white part) is for drug delivery." All of that research project was on effectively injecting medicine into the white part of the eye. Who thinks about that?! We are complex, and we are *fearfully and wonderfully made.*

This book is grounded in biblical anthropology and the understanding of humanity as created beings with physical, psychological, and spiritual components. Anthropology and the pursuit of an understanding of the composition of human beings provides the foundation upon which this book operates. Humans have been studied and classified in an effort to establish how human beings came to be what they are today. Modern science is limited in its ability to define humans because it does not allow for more than can be seen, felt, or heard. Thus, anthropology by itself is merely a foundation, but a more concentrated focus was used for this book.

Anthropology does not fully define a significant approach to human composition because of inherent limitations. Anthropology as a branch of science looks at the heart, organs, blood, sweat, brain, and chemical reactions, ignoring a significant understanding of the intangible nature of humanity. Theological anthropology furthers the understanding of human beings by looking at the relationship between humanity and God, its creator. Biblical anthropology improves the depth of the understanding of humanity by including the Judeo-Christian perspective. This line of thinking culminates in Christian anthropology with the focus on Jesus of Nazareth, the Christ, who personified humanity perfected.

Biblical anthropology differentiates itself from the purely scientific realm at the beginning of the Bible. According to Genesis 2:7: "[T]hen the Lord God formed man from the dust of the ground, and breathed into his nostrils the breath of life; and the man became a living being" (NRSV). Humanity has a body most certainly, but God has also gifted humans with a soul, "the breath of life," which differentiates humanity from the rest of the created realm. Ray S. Anderson explains that humans, as created beings, have a connection to the Creator: "Our existence is tethered to some other source of life, something that makes us always more than mere object, something which posits subjectivity and selfhood as the core of human personhood."[27] Life is about more than being a created being; it involves the relationship with the One who created.

The existence of the body and the soul invites a new discussion: defining which entities comprise the human being. While Christian anthropology suggests that the body and soul are intertwined in some manner, theologians debate how that union functions. Three approaches have been discussed extensively: monist, dichotomist, and trichotomist.

The monistic understanding suggests a unified body and soul without differentiation. The dichotomistic approach proposes the body and soul are separate entities. The trichotomistic view describes a human being as having three parts: body, mind, and spirit. All three proposals do not allow for a human being to be defined without acknowledging the components that comprise the *whole* creature.[28]

The multiple components of human beings define what it is to be human. One cannot begin to understand the composition of a human being without attempting to connect those components in some way. I use a tripartite understanding of humanity: body, soul, and mind. Intentional emphasis on these three components supports a holistic lifestyle, which results in a healthy lifestyle. Lifestyles that pursue wellness of the complete person are not only healthier but are founded on biblical principles and in keeping with God's plan for humanity.

God is trinitarian in nature. From the beginning of time, through the creation story, realized in the life of Christ and culminating in the final judgment, God relates to the world as Father, Son, and Holy Spirit. Genesis 1:26a describes the creation of humanity: "Then God said, 'Let us make humankind in our image, according to our likeness (NRSV)." This collective description (i.e., our image, our likeness) does not describe any other heavenly beings, but that language shows the triune God speaking, acting, and interacting with God's very creation.

Just as God is composed of three distinct but united persons, God's creation, humanity, has a tripartite nature as well. In Matthew 22, Jesus echoes the description from Deuteronomy as

He details the composition of a human being as heart, soul, and mind. Human beings are complete only when the physical, spiritual, and mental components are connected and united in the pursuit of holiness. Jesus further emphasizes this point in Matthew 26:41: "[T]he spirit indeed is willing, but the flesh is weak." By this reference, Jesus is implying that his followers must have both a willing spirit and a strong flesh to be effective Christian disciples. I utilize that principle to assist people in improving their physical wellness.

Christ exemplified the holistic approach with the life he lived but also with the message He provided. Jesus healed a paralytic as recorded in Mark 2:1-12, when Jesus emphasized that the multiple components of the human being must be addressed to achieve wellness: "'But so you may know that the Son of Man has authority on earth to forgive sins'—He said to the paralytic—'I say to you, stand up, take your mat and go to your home'" (Mark 2:10-11, NRSV). Not only did Jesus want to heal him of his physical affliction, but He wanted to reconcile his spirit and improve his spiritual health as well. Jesus' message of holism and humans' search for it is grounded in His own existence.

God has written a message on our hearts like a professional baseball player who signs an autograph on the ball he launched out of the park for a home run. The baseball by itself is not special. There are countless ones produced every year by Rawlings, Spalding, Wilson, and other companies. They are baseballs, but they do not have much value if they are just sitting on the floor. A ball that is in the game...the bigger the game, the more valuable the ball is. When a hall-of-fame batter hits that ball out of the park, and then signs it, that ball is worth a great deal. God has done that for us: we are supremely valuable to God.

While I was at Auburn University working on my MBA, I went to many sporting events. They have a great sports program, and I even had the privilege of working on the staff of Auburn's world-class swim team. The pool shared the parking lot with the baseball stadium, Hitchcock Field at Plainsman Park—where the likes of greats like Bo Jackson, Frank Thomas, and Tim Hudson played college baseball.

One day I was walking by the stadium while a game was taking place. I arrived not too long after a game ball had been launched out of the stadium after being foul-tipped straight back over home plate. I picked it up and saw the mark from the bat and the South Eastern Conference (SEC) logo. I cherish that ball, and I still have it today. God has given us greater gifts than that, and if we can understand His design plan for our bodies, we *can* get healthier.

God's autograph is clear for us and defines who we are to be. God says, I have given you a mind, a body, and a soul; they are yours and they are connected. We need to use all three to fulfill God's plan for us. If we are unhealthy in some part of us, we are *unhealthy* beings because of those connections. God wants us to rebuild—to remove the *unhealth* and restore health to our lives.

Gifted as we are by God to have this tripartite design enables us to find strength in the connections that bind us together. Where one area is weak, we can harness the power in another area to return to wholeness. When one system breaks down, we have a form of redundancy that keeps us functioning and can lead us back to health. We have two eyes, two ears, two kidneys, two arms, two legs, two lungs, … We are designed to take a hit and keep functioning.

When I was finally cleared to begin physical therapy—some three months after my accident—I learned quickly what the plan was. Well, even before I was cleared to begin therapy, I thought about my goals. I knew that I was broken, and I decided—committed myself to the truth—that I was going to work hard to get past this accident toward restoration. There was no other option. I did not allow for an *if* in this conversation. It was more of a question of *when* I was going to get better. I had no idea about specific goals but one day at a time, trying to get better doing what I could for that one day.

Nehemiah had a goal. We even read that he kept it to himself. He didn't want any distractions...anyone telling him he couldn't do it...he shouldn't do it...he wouldn't do it. Nehemiah went about his work to determine what needed to be done:

> So I came to Jerusalem and was there three days. And I arose in the night, I and a few men with me. I did not tell anyone what my God was putting into my mind to do for Jerusalem and there was no animal with me except the animal on which I was riding. So I went out at night by the Valley Gate in the direction of the Dragon's Well and *on* to the Refuse Gate, inspecting the walls of Jerusalem which were broken down and its gates which were consumed by fire. Then I passed on to the Fountain Gate and the King's Pool, but there was no place for my mount to pass. So I went up at night by the ravine and inspected the wall. Then I entered the Valley Gate again and returned. The officials did not know where I had gone or what I had done; nor had I as yet told the Jews, the priests, the nobles,

the officials or the rest who did the work. (Neh. 2:11-16, NASB)

Nehemiah didn't tell anyone what he was doing. Nehemiah says, *there's nothing to see here; ignore this little midnight parade, consisting of me and the fellas. We just feel like a donkey ride...for some fresh air...at night...go back to your houses...we don't want to keep you from your beauty sleep.* They must have thought, how nice; let's go to bed, we'll see him in the morning. Nehemiah had work to do, and he wasn't going to trifle with the people who wanted to get in his way.

Nehemiah goes on his reconnaissance mission, and he sees for himself how bad things are: "the walls of Jerusalem which were broken down and its gates which were consumed by fire" (Neh. 2:13b, NASB). Yep, no confusion now. The walls of Jerusalem were broken down, and gates of the city were consumed by fire.

It's here that we so often see more than we want to see. When we see brokenness, it's enough. Serious unhealth is enough...we don't want to see anymore. No one does. When we are hurting, sometimes we don't want to know how bad it really is, but we cannot stop assessing until we have a full understanding of what is really wrong with us. We cannot hold anything back; God wants access to every...single...part of us. God is not just interested in the good stuff—our talents and abilities. God says, *I want it all— the good and especially the bad. I cannot do anything through you if you do not give me all of you.*

Jesus teaches a great lesson about holding things back. In Luke, we see a rich young man...someone who has only ever achieved in his life. He is successful. He is well-known. He has land. He has authority. He has status. He is a *ruler*, in fact. People know who he is, and everyone notices when he walks into a room. Something is missing, and this young man knows it. There is something deep down that he cannot figure out, nor does he know how to make things right inside.

This is why he comes to Jesus. He wants to stop wanting. People think he has everything, but he knows he has nothing. Jesus sees right through him. We know the type: he has the best clothes, the best watch, the best car, all the women he can date, all the land he could need, and all the business connections he could ever use. He looks the part, and he is in the practice of giving help, not asking for it.

He couldn't stop himself that day. He got up like normal, and he didn't know why, but he made his way to where Jesus was. The crowd was gigantic, but when he approached Jesus, everyone disappeared. He saw only Jesus. It was intimate. It was a powerful moment where anything was possible.

In Luke 18:18b, he asks the big question, "What shall I do to inherit eternal life?" *I am a winner now, but I want to be a winner forever...all eternity. How can I live forever?* Jesus sees through all of the smoke and mirrors. Jesus says, *sure, you are successful, but you are lacking.* Jesus says, "One thing you still lack; sell all that you possess and distribute it to the poor, and you shall have treasure in heaven; and come, follow me" (Luke 18:22, NASB). That's it...that was the one thing. It was too much for him. He was a man who had everything, but he did not have what he needed most.

The rich young ruler was so close to the answer for which he had searched all this time. He knew something was missing, and now he knew how to fix it. But like so many of us, he did not want it bad enough. He would not accept the help that was offered him. God was ready to heal him—to rebuild his life around the correct goals and purpose, but the change was too much for him. He would have to go too far past his comfort zone. *I cannot do anything through you if you do not give me all of you.*

You may be overweight…you may even be obese. That is enough. We can focus on that, and we can attack that problem and go all out to lose weight. But if we don't really get our minds around why that unhealth exists, it will all be for nothing. There are underlying issues that we must understand about why we are inactive or why we can't control what we eat or why the only joy in our life comes from a bottle.

Nehemiah got to a point where he had seen enough. He had lots to do, and he needed to get to work. It was late. His donkey was tired. The parade was getting boring and old, and no one likes a boring parade. They came to a point of destruction that was so bad they couldn't get through. The topography and the desolation was such that the assessment couldn't go on. Nehemiah knew part of what he had to do, but he didn't know everything he had to do.

You know what Nehemiah *didn't* do? He didn't pack it up and head home and get some much-needed sleep. No, he got off the donkey. He got off the donkey, and then we see that he did some rock climbing up a ravine to get a bird's eye view of the situation (Neh. 2:14-15, NASB).

Some of us need to get off of our asses. (It's in the Bible, okay. Ass is another word for a donkey…look it up.) We need to get off of our backsides and really check things out. Then, we need to do some climbing—asking some tough questions—to get the whole picture…to really understand what we are up against.

Sometimes it is our family dysfunction that is working against us. Sometimes we have enemies that are out to get us. Sometimes we sabotage our own efforts because we can't help ourselves. And sometimes it is the Devil himself who is attacking us, weakening us so we cannot be the servants God is calling us to be. We have to walk the entire wall to really understand what we are up against.

When I was leaving the bicycle accident site that morning, I was not alone. I already shared God was with me, but it was more than that. My wife and I had the exact same thought even though we were not actually together. She drove to the accident site, arriving before I left for Augusta. She drove up to the accident scene with multiple vehicles on the side of the road, state and local police cars and multiple ambulances. It did not look good. She ran up in time to see me strapped to the backboard on a gurney in the ambulance. She kissed me, and we said we loved each other. Moments later, we had the thought: I am not dead and I am not paralyzed, so it could be a lot worse. It's going to be okay. She comforted herself: *He's alive and he can talk to me, so we will be alright.*

That sounds sweet and all, but that can't get you through the tough times…or can it? My recovery process was extensive. It was not the worst you've ever heard of, nor was it a walk in the park. (I couldn't actually walk, so there's that.) After a few days in the hospital following the accident, I was discharged. We have some great friends who are in trucking and shipping. My wife and I figured they would be the ones to call: if they can handle hazardous materials and precious commodities, they could be trusted with a broken-up preacher.

My big problem, besides the four fractures in my leg, was my broken back and damaged SI (sacroiliac) joint: I could not sit. I don't mean it didn't feel good. I mean I COULD NOT sit. They were able to help me kind of lay down in the backseat of the cab of a pickup truck. When we got home, I tried to lay on the couch.

That lasted about 15 seconds. Even with my back brace on, that did not work.

A familiar theme for us was the great people who took care of us. Friends who own a pharmacy and hospital supply store let us borrow a hospital bed, which became my new home for the next six weeks. I was told to stay on my back, only getting up to go to the bathroom. That simple task was even too precarious for weeks after the accident because of the concussion side effects and the damaged leg that had not been repaired.

Finally came surgery for my leg. I wasn't allowed to work for a while, and I could not begin physical therapy for at least 10 weeks after surgery. I was ready to do something—anything—proactive or productive to the healing process.

Nehemiah tells us that he did not tell anyone what he was doing. He went on his journey around the wall, checking and inspecting with the few men who were with him. They were probably servants who were REAL excited to be out in the middle of the night observing architecture by the light of a torch. Nehemiah gained clarity on how bad the situation really was. Still, he told no one what he was going to do.

We learn that Nehemiah had a plan. He knew how he was going to do things. He just needed to know what the scope of his project was going to be. He had picked his workforce (the Jews, the priests, the officials, and the laborers). Now he had to do the work.

After my surgery and as my back began to heal, I was waiting (sometimes impatiently) for physical therapy to begin. I began to crutch everywhere. I crutched up and down the street we lived on, just to get my blood moving and to breathe some fresh air. I do 77 push-ups every morning…EVERY morning. (Whether I am well or not; hurting; tired; sick; whatever. It is how I start my day, every day.) I figured early on, I needed to keep that going. So, I would crutch to a spot, and support myself on my good leg and do my push-ups. I started back a few weeks into my recovery.

This was a difficult battle I was waging. I lost so much muscle mass and tone from lying around. Before the accident (or when I became a hood ornament), I weighed 162lbs. In a matter of weeks, I was down to 147lbs. at my lowest. I had ministered to enough hospital patients to know, I had to force myself to eat every day…three meals a day. Regardless of whether I wanted to eat or not, I had to eat for strength. So, I ate meals I did not want, three times a day.

To get better, you must set up a structure and repeat and repeat and repeat. Stick with the plan. My old swim coach at the Naval Academy, Lee Lawrence, helped us with race strategy. I was a distance swimmer, and our races were long…like the 800m and 400m, both events of which I had to swim in our dual meets. When preparing for a race, coach would tell us to set our hand speed and let it carry us through the race. The idea is if you start out too fast with your hands pulling under you through the water (your propulsion) you will burn out and crack in a long race. If you start out too slowly, you won't be able to catch up or make up the distance lost. If you can set your hand speed at a pace that you can sustain, you will swim as fast as you can and hopefully win the race.

When Nehemiah saw the condition of the wall, he could have given up. When you and I see how far off target we have gotten— how deep into unhealth we have gone—we can give up. It can seem too daunting, and it may make more sense for us to relish in our brokenness and just get used to it. We can wallow in the quagmire of our destruction and never get better. When the terrain got rough and Nehemiah could not go any further, he didn't give up. Just as Nehemiah didn't rend his garments, put on sackcloth, and put ashes on his head, neither should we. We are only a serious commitment away from being healthier.

Our minds are extremely powerful, but they have to be utilized correctly. That's what structure and a plan can do for us. Dr. Caroline Leaf taught at Catalyst Atlanta in 2014, and she explained to us that the mind is separate than the body. It is its own entity. The mind tells the brain what to do, because the brain is an organ of the body like the heart or the stomach. If our mind commits to doing something our body tries to figure out how to do it.

When I started back to running, which was hard to actually call *running*, it was more like awkward shuffling because of how odd I looked. Making my body work correctly was harder than I ever could have imagined. I lost range of motion in my rebuilt ankle—like, it couldn't do what it used to be able to do. My mind told my brain, *we are going to run now*. My brain and my body had to figure out a way to follow that command. It looked like my legs were running sideways to make myself go forward. It wasn't pretty, but I was running. My mind gave the command, and my body followed.

There is strength in routine. If we set our minds to doing something, the rest of us figures out a way to do it. Nehemiah was going to have to lean on a routine and a process to get the work done. In the next chapter, we will see just what Nehemiah set his mind to, in order to reach his goal.

CHAPTER 4

DO WHAT IT TAKES

DESTIN SANDLIN IS AN engineer who educates people on the Internet with his "Smarter Every Day" series. His "The Backwards Brain Bicycle" episode explains how Destin re-learned to ride a bicycle. A welder in his shop decided to mess with him and reversed the steering on a bicycle by adding some cogs at the base of the handlebars: when the handlebars turn to the right, the front wheel turns to the left, and when the handlebars turn to the left, the front wheel turns to the right. Sounds simple enough, right? But when Sandlin tried to ride the bike, he absolutely could not.

Sandlin goes on to explain the process of learning to ride that particular bike. We have all heard the saying, "It's just like riding a bike." But this bike is different. Sandlin has been riding a bike for most of his life—some 30 years, but he can't ride a bike anymore… not a normal bike anyway.

Sandlin proved something amazing about our minds. We can rewire our brains, even changing a process we have known as normal and second nature for our entire lives. When Sandlin attempted to ride the altered bike, he…could…not…do…it. (I would wager, if I wagered, that you and I could not do it either.) Sandlin realized that he had the knowledge of how to ride a bike but not the understanding (knowledge ≠ understanding). So, he began the journey to change his understanding.

Sandlin practiced riding the bicycle every day for five minutes a day. He crashed. He looked silly. He struggled. It took him eight months, but it happened. One day he could not ride the bike, and the next day he could. But it wasn't like riding his old bike. If there was any distraction from his focus, his brain would default back to its prior programming and he would lose the ability. Finally, he mastered the bike, and he didn't have to focus—it became normal.

Next, it was time for a test. Sandlin tried to ride a regular bike. Once again, he…could…not…do…it. After 20 minutes of trying, the switch flipped, and he could ride a regular bike again.²⁹ That wasn't the point. We can retrain our brains. You and I can rebuild our lives. We can become healthier. The amount of information available about health, dieting, and fitness is staggering, but knowledge ≠ understanding. We have to decide we are going to be better.

> Then I said to them, 'You see the bad situation we are in, that Jerusalem is desolate and its gates burned by fire. Come, let us rebuild the wall of Jerusalem so that we will no longer be a reproach.' I told them how the hand of my God had been favorable to me and also about the king's words which he had spoken to me. Then they said, "Let us arise and build." So they put their hands to the good work. (Neh. 2:17-18, NASB)

Nehemiah had to be one heck of a leader. This is it. Those two verses describe what Nehemiah said to a group of his future workers—the physical labor he needed to rebuild Jerusalem. He didn't promise them a seat next to God. He didn't tell them they would help rule Jerusalem. Nor, did he tell them you have to help me do this or God will rain down fire on your heads. No, Nehemiah decided to go the straightforward route and it worked.

He gave them a reality check: things are bad; the wall is destroyed; the city is desolate; and I just walked the whole thing and you can't even get around the rubble on foot. In his short speech, Nehemiah doesn't use *I* and *you* language; it is all about the *we*. "Let's do this, so *we* won't be a disgrace…so that *we* won't make God look bad…so that *we* will have a home that honors God once again."

If we are unhealthy—there is some part of our holistic being that is out of whack—we need to realize how that reflects on us, not in the minds of others, but to God. God created us to be perfect, but sin makes that nearly impossible. I say *nearly impossible* because it takes the perfecting, or *sanctifying*, work of God in the person of the Holy Spirit to overcome the damage of sin.

Our goal is, simply, to grow into the image of Jesus Christ. That is what God desires for all of us: to be healthy spiritually, physically, and mentally. God loves us. God never stops coming after us. No matter how corrupted we are by sin and its lust, greed, self-centeredness, and hatred, God still comes after us to save us and make us better. That's what Jesus was and is: the template for us to be healthy. With that in mind, it might help to look to Jesus for assistance.

No human being better personified what we were created to be than Jesus of Nazareth. While being fully human, Jesus was also fully divine, but the example He provided was for all humanity to follow. The Gospel of John explains the threefold dimension of Jesus' Incarnation in the world: "And the Word became flesh and lived among us, and we have seen his glory, the glory as of a father's only son, full of grace and truth" (John 1:14, NASB). The Son of God put on flesh to dwell on earth and provide humanity with the understanding of communion with God—union and connection with the Creator.

In that one verse from John about the life of the living Word, Jesus is described physically, mentally, and spiritually. Firstly, the physical nature of Jesus is seen as He "became flesh and lived among us": that is, He lived a life and breathed air in and out. He walked on the earth, engaging with family members, followers, enemies, and disciples. John was a follower of Jesus and worked with Him during His ministry on earth and after He was resurrected from the dead, and he saw the example that Jesus lived. Because of the witness Jesus the Christ provided, John said, "[W]e have seen His glory."

Secondly, John explains that Jesus lived a life full of grace, showing the world what spiritual connection with God is. Without a connection to God our Creator, we are never fully human ourselves. He provided an example, as detailed in the life of Jesus described in Scripture, of what a life of grace looks like and how it flows from the heart of God through the hearts of men and women.

Thirdly, John explains that Jesus was full of truth, the words Jesus shared and the message He fashioned with His mind and mental abilities. Jesus saw the world as it was and knew what it was supposed to be. He spoke into the world around Him to instruct and teach and declare who we were supposed to be. His words were truth, and Jesus lived that truth. Only through these three facets of his earthly existence, can humanity appreciate the validity and necessity of living life in the holistic manner Jesus did.

The life of Jesus as detailed in the narrative accounts in the New Testament of the Bible provides further understanding of the holistic, incarnational life—God living and working through us as willing partners. Jesus is the prototype for how humanity is to encounter life fully with the presence of God indwelling them. The incarnational life…or the *God with us* life…is further described in John 17.

In this discourse, Jesus prayed to God just before he was betrayed into the hands of the earthly authorities. Jesus prayed that His followers would "all be one" and that they would be united with God as Jesus was (John 17:20-22, NASB). In this prayer Jesus states what the incarnational existence is to be for humanity. He described the goal for humanity while detailing the gravity of the witness they provide:

> The glory that You have given Me I have given them, so that they may be one, as We are one, I in them and You in Me, that they may become completely one, so that the world may know that You have sent Me and have loved them even as You have loved Me. (John 17:22-23)

The goal is for humanity to be united with God and live incarnationally, and the *God with us life* witnesses to the world the validity of the ministry of Jesus. *God with us living* shows the world God's love and real presence as it works through us making us more like Jesus.

The Word becomes flesh and dwells in the hearts of humanity, but the presence of God in humanity is not solely a personal encounter. Jesus attempted to explain to His antagonists what life on earth would look like as followers of the living God. To catch Jesus in a trap, the Jewish authorities asked Jesus which of the Ten Commandments was the greatest and most important law to follow. That would be like asking someone today who is the greatest basketball player: Michael Jordan, Kobe Bryant, or LeBron James? Any answer brings both a valid opinion and real outrage. Let's be clear…M.J. is the greatest basketball player in the history of the world…or in the world to come. Jesus was asked which commandment was the greatest, to which Jesus responded with an answer that was beyond what his enemies could have anticipated:

> The first is, "Hear, O Israel: the Lord our God, the Lord is one; you shall love the Lord your God with all your heart, and with all your soul, and with all your mind, and with all your strength." The second is this, "You shall love your neighbor as yourself." There is no other commandment greater than these. (Mark 12:29-31, NASB)

Jesus avowed that human beings were to worship God holistically with their souls, minds, and bodies.

M. Robert Mulholland, Jr. suggests that the message Jesus conveys is not a hierarchical response as a more modern reading would suggest, but an explanation of the Deuteronomical commandment. Mulholland maintains that the *second* commandment is just another way to express the sentiment in the *first* commandment. He explains the incarnational nature of Jesus' followers: "The context of our relationship with God is our relationship with others."[30] This reality places true importance on the life of each human being, and it commends the outward life as a reflection of the inward life.

Anderson similarly describes humanity by contrasting humans with other created things. He suggests that the "human creature" is attached to the "other," and this connection allows humanity to exist as more than an object. A personhood is established that separates the human creature from other creatures. Anderson describes the relationship: "I am embodied soul and ensouled body. Apart from my human soul, my body is merely a material object and thus impersonal. But also apart from my body, my soul is elusive and abstract and just as impersonal."[31] For Anderson, the human existence is a question of life as an object or a subject, and he concludes that the connection with God validates the subjectivity of life and explains why the soul and body are necessarily joined.

The outward life of faith is a reflection of the presence of God. In Matthew's account of the beginning of Jesus' ministry, He was baptized by John the Baptist, and then He saw the Spirit of God descend like a dove upon Him. The Spirit then led Him into the wilderness (Matt. 3:13-4:25, NASB). This time in the wilderness was a chance for Jesus to experience the power of the Spirit and the temptations of the flesh. He fasted for forty days and forty nights, and then the devil came to Him when He was *famished* in His physical weakness. Weakness is a state in which the human condition is exposed and at risk for attack from the evil one. The soul can be famished as well, but Jesus taught His disciples, even in the midst of attack.

The devil came to Jesus, speaking firstly to His physical condition of hunger. The body is the vehicle of the soul, connected and intertwined. When tempted with the idea to make bread from stones, Jesus cited Deuteronomy 8:3: "It is written, one does not live by bread alone, but by every word that comes from the mouth of God" (Matt. 4:4, NRSV). Jesus implied that sustenance for physical existence is important, but the nourishment God provides the soul is primary. Secondly, the devil dared Jesus to prove His Lordship by throwing himself off the top of the temple, allowing angels to save him. Jesus declared that one should not use the body with which they are gifted as a means to test the Lord God.

Thirdly, the devil tempted Jesus with all of the success and power the created world could offer by removing His allegiance from God and worshipping another. Jesus, in His threefold response to temptation, declared that humanity is sustained by what God alone provides, spiritually and physically. Jesus answered correctly, and "then the devil left him, and suddenly angels came and waited on him" (Matt. 4:11, NRSV). With the declaration of His faith, his temptation abated, and he was validated.

Jesus was once again vindicated at His resurrection. After He was brutally tortured and murdered, His physical body failed Him and He died. With the perception of His ministry in shambles, Jesus was resurrected, not in a spiritual manner or as a ghost, but in His physical body once again. In Luke's account, Jesus appeared to His followers and confirmed his body was resurrected: "Look at My hands and My feet; see that it is I Myself. Touch Me and see; for a ghost does not have flesh and bones as you see that I have" (Luke 24:39, NRSV). To confirm what they were seeing, Jesus asked for something to eat, and then He ate some broiled fish. Jesus is the Son of God, and in His divinity and humanness He shows that God's creation is perfected in the union of the physical, spiritual, and mental realms. The new birth from above does not end with death and is consummated with the resurrection of the body.

With the knowledge from witnessing the life, death, resurrection, and ascension of Jesus, His followers provide a keen perspective and revelation of the lives disciples of Jesus are to live. Their writings and letters provided the foundation for soteriology—the path of salvation—and the praxis of the Christian life. Those closest to Jesus shed significant light on how the Christian faith should manifest itself. Peter writes of the need to engage all aspects of life as part of the new birth and salvation through Jesus:

> Therefore prepare your minds for action; discipline yourselves; set all your hope on the grace that Jesus Christ will bring you when He is revealed. Like obedient children, do not be conformed to the desires that you formerly had in ignorance. Instead, as He who called you is holy, be holy yourselves in all your conduct; for it is written, "You shall be holy, for I am holy." (1 Pet. 1:13-16, NRSV)

Peter exhorts that the mental approach to life is vital to salvation, and he calls for a disciplined existence. Peter says holiness is the calling for disciples of Jesus, and he affirms the holistic experience of the mind, the body, and the soul.

Paul also writes about the *God with us* nature of the body of Christ, and his understanding helped shape the early Christian Church. While not a follower of Jesus during Jesus' earthly ministry, Paul was still an Apostle. He was a prolific writer who ministered to many churches, and he sought to build them up and correct them when needed. Some confusion does exist around Paul's view of the holistic approach to life. At times, in Paul's letters, the physical realm seems to be described in opposition to the spiritual and mental realms.

However, if one were to look at Paul's collection of works, a consistency of thought around the holistic existence is evident. When Paul is concluding his letter to the church in Rome, he summarizes his ministry in the Eastern Mediterranean region as a reliance on incarnational living:

> For I will not venture to speak of anything except what Christ has accomplished through me to win obedience from the Gentiles, by word and deed, by the power of signs and wonders, by the power of the Spirit of God, so that from Jerusalem and as far as around Illyricum I have proclaimed the good news of Christ. (Rom. 15:18-19, NRSV)

Paul professes a life confirmed by other texts in the New Testament, including his own writings. A life of faith is a life of word and deed.

Paul wrote profusely to churches to inspire them to live their faith by word and deed. He called for orthopraxis—right living—and looked for signs of their faith through many avenues, including monetary offerings to the larger church community. While Paul called for faith in action, some look to his letters and find validation of a concept contrary to the tenor of Scripture and the life of Jesus represented in the Gospels. Paul is cited in support of those who believe that the flesh and the spirit are in opposition to each other.

Paul writes in Romans about salvation and whether justification comes by works or by faith. Paul explains that justification occurs as a result of faith alone and not works, and in that discourse, *the flesh* is discussed. Plato had a tremendous influence on many in the Hellenistic world of the first century, as well as in the ages that followed, through his theories on the composition of human life. E. A. Livingstone attempts to define Platonic thought, which holds that the soul is captured by the body and they are in opposition to each other: "This contrasts the world of sense and everyday experience with the true or higher world of 'Ideas' (or better, 'Forms')."[32] Thus, what the body is and what is perceived through the tangible arena limits the elevation of the mind and soul. This belief that salvation is a freeing of the soul from the body is contrary to the message of Jesus, but this approach to spirituality was rampant in the world in which the early Church functioned.

Paul would have been aware of Plato, but Paul's understanding of the flesh was different from that of Plotinus and the third century Neoplatonist movement. Anthony Meredith summarizes the Neoplatonist philosophy and that of Plotinus, emphasizing the extension of parts of Plato's model. Plotinus continued much of Plato's conversations but not all of his teachings. While politics was not to his interest, Plotinus furthered the work of Plato on the Forms. Plotinus divided the discussion into three groups: the One, the Mind, and the Soul. Enlightenment was the source of transcendence, a return to the One from which life emanates. Plotinus theorized that human reason was the vehicle necessary to return the Soul to the One.[33] Undoubtedly, Neoplatonist thought influenced the early Church, though not the authors of the biblical text. However, the confusion that trickled down through history came from those who interpreted Paul's biblical letters in light of the Neoplatonist theories.

The Soul vs. the Body fight has been raging for some time, and it is still alive in our culture today. We see it very often in movies as the hangover of *Gnostic* thought is still a part of our society without actually being named. The *Gnostics* sprang up after Jesus' Ascension and as Jewish, Christian, and Greek cultures merged and meshed. *Gnosis* is Greek for knowledge, and they believed there was a secret about Jesus that only they knew.

Heavily influenced by Plato and Greek philosophy, the *Gnostics* believed in Jesus, but not as Christian orthodoxy knows Jesus. *Gnostics* believed the flesh—our body—is sinful and cannot be anything other than that. Conversely, they believed our soul was pure and holy. In their minds, each of us was a walking bird cage: our body is the cage and our soul is the bird waiting to be freed. This freedom would come when the body died, and only then could we be free of sin.

The theological fight came as the Early Church established what exactly Jesus had taught, what they were to believe, and how they were to live. *Gnostics* were considered heretics—*non*-orthodox believers, because they said if Jesus was God—pure—He could not have corrupted Himself with actual flesh. Jesus must have been a spirit, and He only looked like a human. He couldn't have died on the cross, so He just looked like He did. His passion and death were all a drama played out to confuse the authorities. This goes against a key belief of Christians: Jesus is fully God and fully human. As far-fetched as *Gnosticism* sounds (and they have way more beliefs about Jesus that sound like mythology), their beliefs permeates our culture.

Hollywood produces movies all of the time that are *Gnostic* in nature. The movie "Inception" came out in 2010 with Leonardo DiCaprio playing the lead role. They told a story that was dominated by time spent living hundreds, if not, thousands of years in their minds with their bodies in a drug-induced coma-like state.

While that is the most recent, popular example, one series takes the cake for being influenced by *Gnosticism*.

"The Matrix" came out in 1999; there were two other Matrix movies in the franchise following the original blockbuster, completing the trilogy. With Christocentric language throughout the movie (characters named Trinity, the Architect, the Oracle, the One, and an aircraft named *Logos*—the Greek name for Jesus in the Early Church), *Gnostic* thought was fully engaged in the script writing and storyline.

In the movie, human beings exist as batteries to supply energy to machines, who have taken over the world. Their whole life is spent in individual pods, being fed through a hose and existing in an unconscious state. Human brains are engaged through the mental connection via a cable to a computer program called *the Matrix*, hence the title of the movies. Nearly all of the human population lives out their life as a *copper-top*, a movie reference to Duracell batteries. Once you receive the higher knowledge—*gnosis*—you can escape the Matrix and return to the computer program as anything you desire. You simply download the information to your brain, and then you can do what you want. Their bodies are reclined and lifeless, while their brains are living an exciting and even ideal life. This sounds a little too close to the existence of many of our species today and not what God intended for us.

Paul's understanding of the *flesh* in Romans bears discussion because flesh can be interpreted in a similar manner as a sensory experience seen in platonic thought. Paul references the *flesh* multiple times in Romans 8, but its use does not involve the flesh and blood of humanity. Paul is referring to flesh as humanity's propensity to sin. That passage in Romans is part of a larger conversation from Paul about salvation and justification in the eyes of God in spite of the weakening of flesh, or sin. Paul explains, "[F]or if you live according to the flesh, you will die; but if by the Spirit you put to death the deeds of the body, you will live" (Rom. 8:13, NRSV). The New International Version is more accurate in its translation as the death of "misdeeds." Paul exhorts consistently to respond to the good news of Jesus with word and deed. Paul understands humanity to be sinful inherently, but not everything human beings do is corrupt.

Paul further clarifies his belief in the connection among body, mind, and soul in 1 Thessalonians. As Paul ends the letter to this church, he clearly is not writing a systematic approach to sin and salvation as in Romans. Paul is writing to fellow disciples of Jesus, and he believes they are not living according to misdeeds or to satisfy carnal urges but to be made holy. Paul reminds them of who they are:

> For this is the will of God, your sanctification: that you abstain from fornication; that each one of you know how to control your own body in holiness and honor, not with lustful passion, like the Gentiles who do not know God. (1 Thess. 4:3-5, NRSV)

Paul suggests that with God in their lives, present in the person of the Holy Spirit, they are equipped with the means to defend themselves against misdeeds and sins and to live lives in the manner of Jesus. They are being sanctified because of Jesus, the "forerunner of faith," and just as he was God incarnate, so, too, is God similarly dwelling in each of them. Paul's emphasis on the holistic life is still misunderstood by some, and confusion can be detrimental to the life of faith.

Further analysis of Paul's letters reveals evidence to support Anderson and his rejection of a disembodied existence. Second Corinthians 5:4 details Paul's fear of disembodiment: "For while we are still in this tent, we groan under our burden, because we wish not to be unclothed but to be further clothed, so that what is mortal may be swallowed up by life." Anderson suggests that Paul is describing disembodiment, the soul separated from the body. This point returns the conversation to Anderson's view of personhood as a subject, not object. He reinforces his position: "Therefore, we conclude that it is unnatural for the human person to experience separation of the soul and body, for it leads to a depersonalization of the self."[34] Anderson's position is clear on the issue of life and afterlife, but the transition between those two states requires discussion.

Joel B. Green suggests that Paul provides the standard needed to understand the flesh and the idea of sanctification, or perfection, through relationship with God. He discusses this relationship through the concept of "soteriological wholism" (Brown, Murphy, and Maloney 28). Wholism is a matter of human beings being related to others and God as a condition of salvation. Nancey Murphy proposes that "nonreductive physicalism" is the approach that is most in agreement with Christian teaching. The physicality of humanity ties all of the functioning together in the moral and spiritual realms while interaction with God serves as the substance that binds the systems together (25). Green agrees with much of Murphy's approach, and he references two different accounts from the New Testament to demonstrate the relatedness of which he is focused.

In 1 Corinthians 15:38-58, Paul writes about the resurrection of the body. Green suggests that Paul is exhorting people of different societal classes and educational backgrounds, seeking to explain life after death. Multiple readers may have some difficulty arriving at the same conclusion about Paul's message, but Green sees continuity across Pauline texts. Green suggests Paul sees a strong connection between the present life and the life to come, and the bodily existence is the link (170-71). Green explains that Paul is not looking for a resuscitation of a dead body or the immortality of a soul. God transforms the body, much like the example of Jesus, and salvation is defined through such a divine and supernatural initiative.

Rudolph Bultmann sees this same passage from 1 Corinthians 15 in a different light, and he recommends another reason for the confusion around the message of the *body*. Bultmann explains the confusion by suggesting that, in this passage, Paul tries to discuss the body/soul connection using the manner and imagery of those who were arguing against him and his view of humanity. Bultmann also proposes additional hindrances to the discussion because of the words available: "The most comprehensive term which Paul uses to characterize man's existence is *soma*, body; it is also the most complex and the understanding of it is fraught with difficulty."[35] He addresses the idea that Paul uses *soma* to refer to the "form" of a body, and he argues that Paul's use of *soma* is in the manner of the "whole person" (192).

In fact, Bultmann declares that Paul never uses *soma* in reference to a corpse, nor does he write of *soma* serving as a kind of prison. Bultmann provides many examples evaluating Pauline text and his usage of *soma* to reach those conclusions, but the amount of material cited is beyond the scope of this book and detracts from its intent. Paul uses *soma* in a consistent manner and as a descriptor of the human condition as a unified whole.

Paul does not agree with the Gnostic understanding of the body, nor does he have any visions of Jesus as the character Neo or the viability of "The Matrix" to explain human existence! I'm a big fan of the trilogy, but even I do not believe we see the true relationship between God and humans in the films. (I am certain my wife, Lindsey, sure doesn't, and I know she is tired of hearing about the movies. And she may be more than a little annoyed I taught my kids the line, "There is no spoon." Oh, well.)

To understand better the relationship between God and humanity regarding the issue of unity, Green moves from the understanding of bodily transformation to an example from Luke 8:42-48 and the hemorrhaging woman. This well-known passage describes a woman who is made whole physically while also soteriologically. Green contends that Jesus not only heals this woman and restores her relationship with God, but Jesus made sure that the crowd knew what had happened. Jesus expressed the necessity for her to be made whole and that her relationship with her brothers and sisters, exemplifying all of humanity, was affirmed and restored.[36] The focus is not a matter of how the soul and body are connected but that they are seen as part of the same being, neither fully existing without the other.

Why would we focus on one part over another? If God wants us to be healthy, or at least as healthy as we can be, why not try to be healthy? So often we take the easy route. We have the innate ability to be our own worst enemy and let ourselves off the hook. *Sure, one doughnut is good, but two would be really good. I know I shouldn't eat late at night, but I'll work it off in my sleep. I need to go to bed earlier, but I really want to watch this movie trilogy I have seen 20 times before until 2 a.m., and try to function tomorrow.* What we do as followers of Jesus matters—in all aspects of life.

When the Ashley Madison scandal happened, I learned a great deal about people. First, it is a scandal that a website designed to connect like-minded married people who want casual affairs exists. But, what surprised me was the disparity seen in the ramifications for clergy and laity caught up in the affairs. Clergy were given no grace when exposed. I know a pastor who was removed from his job in a matter of days and *encouraged* to retire immediately. There was another beloved pastor in Mississippi who committed suicide when people found out. There is a double standard.

I know your first response is, well, clergy are different: they are supposed to be held to a higher standard. I agree with that, but I wonder why laity extend themselves more grace. They are basically suggesting that clergy are parents and laity are toddlers. This just reinforces the idea that followers of Jesus can't really be expected to live to a higher standard. I argue that all followers should be the adults, who know what to do and are setting the examples for non-followers.

This is the transformation Paul talks about in Ephesians 4:14-15 when he says "We are no longer to be children, tossed here and there by waves…we are to grow up in all aspects into Him who is the head, even Christ" (NASB). We actually start holding ourselves to a higher standard and do not let ourselves off the hook so easily. We need grace. We will make mistakes, but we make mistakes trying to be better. We need accountability, and that (probably) may need to come through other people who care for us. When we settle into unhealth—neglecting exercise, having no regard for what we eat, ignoring God and His disciplines and ignoring the development and maintenance of our minds—we are choosing to live like toddlers who don't know any better. That is not what God wants for us.

Nehemiah doesn't end his recruitment speech with the reality check of how bad the wall is and the state of the nation. He goes on to tell them who is calling them to this good work and who will sustain them through it. It is God that called them to this good work, and it is God who calls us out of our unhealthy lifestyles to wellness.

No task is too great for God. We serve a God who acts in this world. John Wesley said, "God does nothing except in response to believing prayer." This means God is waiting on us to pray, and it means God will not act unless we pray expectantly for His intervention. It DOES NOT mean that God is a vending machine where we select what we want and bang the machine when our heart's desire gets hung up on the way down to our hand. Nor does it mean God is a slot machine waiting for the right combination of coins to pay off. Paul tells us, the Holy Spirit directs our prayer, telling us what to pray for with sighs too deep for words (Rom. 8:26, NASB).

If we only depended on our thoughts and desires to guide our prayers, we would be like a child in a candy store. Pastor Mark Batterson from National Community Church in Washington, D.C. has an illuminating understanding of prayer. Batterson declares praying a request to God has a two-fold test. The answer to the prayer must bring God glory and be in the will of God for it to be answered. His understanding is not only about the divine inspiration in our prayer life but also about its efficacy. Make no mistake, living a healthy life—body, mind, and soul—brings God glory and is in His will for us.

Just in my church, I have seen God working in this way. We have the same concerns as many of you: cancer, heart disease, illnesses, strokes, sick children, life direction, … We had a couple who had a baby three weeks early, and before he was even three weeks old, he got very sick. He was rushed to GRUMC in Augusta, GA, which was over an hour away. His heart had swollen, and they were concerned he was going to die: the doctor's estimations were very grave. He had a virus that had gone unnoticed as it attacked his heart, and he had a 1/3 chance that he would have a heart transplant. The Holy Spirit guided us to pray, and our church began to pray for healing. We prayed that the medicine would work, and we prayed that his heart would go back to its normal size. God responded in what the doctors said was a miraculous way. His heart did go back to normal in just a few weeks, and now he is doing well and thriving, years later.

If we listen for God, we can hear the prayers God wants us to pray. We had another family in our church who had a hard time. They had relatives who were sick and battling serious disease. We lost some of those battles and won others. But the parents were dealing with their own health issues, when their daughter got sick. So, we prayed for her, her doctors, and her healing. While I was praying one morning in my devotion time, God told me to pray for her brother, who was barely three years old. I didn't know why, but I did what I was told and I added him to my daily prayers. The next day, their mother called me and told me he was sick and needed surgery.

For weeks, doctors had been chasing the pain of the older sister. They were told it was cancer, then multiple sclerosis, muscular dystrophy. They didn't know what was wrong. Finally they realized it was a disorder affecting her enzyme levels. The disorder causes a reaction with anesthesia and other medicines. Well, they could live with that; she didn't have any surgeries scheduled. The doctors then said it could be genetic, so more tests.

They tested her brother, and they found he had the same exact condition. That is when we all got chill bumps! That is why God had directed me to pray for him. His sister had gone through all of that discomfort and those tests to save her brother's life. If he had had the surgery before they knew about his condition, he would have most likely died on the operating table. He did have extensive surgery, but with the appropriate anesthesia regarding his disorder, he is doing well now. God is amazing and extremely powerful!

Pray. Listen for God. What is God asking you to do? What is God asking you to pray for in regards to some aspect of your life that is unhealthy? That is where we need to begin.

I did my doctoral work with clergy. I developed this system called *Exerceo Divina*. The project involved an intervention to improve the well-being of clergy in the Statesboro District of the South Georgia Conference of the UMC. Their supervisor—district superintendent—conducted meetings every other month with the district clergy at a church in the geographical area to disseminate information, share in interpersonal interactions, and commune for fellowship. With access to the clergy volunteers granted by the district superintendent, the intervention took place between two of the described meetings.

At the initial meeting, I was allotted time for data gathering and a presentation. Two nurses recorded medical diagnostic measurements to contribute data useful in evaluating physical well-being: heart rate, blood pressure, and height and weight measurements for BMI. Two instruments evaluated the self-selected participants' pre-test physical and spiritual well-being—the University of Michigan's Health Risk Appraisal and the Spiritual Well-Being Scale. The volunteers completed the two instruments in thirty minutes.

Following the completion of the instruments, I provided the participants with a booklet I prepared with suggestions for an exercise program and an explanation on how to incorporate *lectio divina* into an exercise program. *Lectio divina* is probably thousands of years old, and it is an approach to reading Scripture, which is more than just reading. It involves *lectio* (reading and re-reading and even memorization of the text), *meditatio* (internalization of the written word), *oratio* (responsive prayer, listening for God's voice and message from the text), and *contemplatio* (union with God).

The program is a four-step process that is akin to walking up stairs to a special room. Maybe you remember a time as a child when you visited with your grandparents, family members, or close friends. There was something special about that time, and there was a special space—room, yard, or seat at a table—that became more than a physical experience. The experience was more than simply *being* somewhere.

Every year from my birth to sometime in my mid-twenties, my family and I would travel to LA...that's right...Lower Alabama. My dad is from LA, and we would spend Christmas at his sister's house with her family and my grandmother. All of those formative Christmas celebrations took place at Kitty-Bubber's house—my aunt and uncle. I can see their living room with a large Christmas tree, decorations, Hershey's Kisses tree, and wonderfully-wrapped presents. That space was truly more than a room in a house; it is a place where life happened and memories were made.

People experience each other on a daily basis, but those special moments are pregnant with opportunity and life-change. You can probably see such a space and remember what those moments can be like. If the people we shared those moments with are gone, the memories allow us to transcend our current reality to be with them once again.

This is how *lectio divina* works. We engage the Creator by reading His message to us—Holy Scripture. We seek understanding of a section, or passage, of the Bible. We talk with God, praying for understanding, about what He is saying to us as the reader at that particular moment in time. Then, we do what many of us do not normally do well, we wait. We wait for God to speak to us. We walk into that old living room and experience a connection with God. *Lectio divina* is a wonderful means to connect with God and a great way to begin or nurture transformation.

During the instructional time of the meeting, along with the instruction on exercise and *lectio divina*, I also discussed ways to make dietary improvements and provided suggestions on how to make healthier food choices. The participants were informed that they would be evaluated again in two months.

During the intervention period, I corresponded with the participants at the two, four, six, and eight-week points to encourage and motivate them. After the intervention period, I again met with the participants at a district meeting. The nurses recorded the same diagnostic measurements. I administered the Health Risk Appraisal and the Spiritual Well-Being Scale a second time for the posttest data. I then conducted a focus group discussion of the intervention to record what portions of the intervention the participants found to be positive or negative influences on their overall well-being.

The participants were on their own without oversight from me to use the plan proposed in the project for the two-month period. They participated in the intervention and incorporated the program into their daily lives to varying degrees. This approach provided the participants with a foundation for change and confidence that they could effectively improve their well-being and impact a long-term correction to an area of their lives that needed improvement.

The results showed that using the *Exerceo Divina* plan does improve health. The participants showed statistically significant improvement in systolic blood pressure (the upper number that correlates with the pumping of the heart) as well as significant improvement in diastolic blood pressure (the lower number that corresponds with the heart at rest). Even an unhealthy group like clergy, got healthier focusing on God's word and exercising. There are no lost causes.

Nehemiah had support for his gigantic task (what others in Judea *knew* was a lost cause), but he also had dissent. They didn't even give him a night to think about it. The haters didn't have a tweak or a suggestion; they just did what haters do: hate. "But when Sanballat the Horonite and Tobiah the Ammonite official, and Geshem the Arab heard it, they mocked us and despised us and said, "What is this thing you are doing? Are you rebelling against the king?" (Neh. 2:19, NASB).

My first thought when I read about Sanballat, Tobiah, and Geshem is of *The Three Stooges*. Sanballat, Tobiah, and Geshem—Moe, Larry, and Curly. I loved the Stooges. I have watched every episode of their inept hijinks. In each episode, there seems to be a logical plan or story that somehow ALWAYS goes awry.

An episode titled "Disorder in the Court" begins with a woman on trial for her life. She is being prosecuted for a murder she didn't commit. The star witness for the defense is Curly. If you ever find yourself in that position, find another witness. Curly and the boys make a mockery of the court being unable to even enter the courtroom or take the oath without incident. Eventually after seeming to be supporting the prosecution, they discover key evidence that frees the suspect. As the newspaper photographer tries to take a picture, making them heroes for all to see, they bust a firehose that ruins the whole scene. Typical.

So much of what Nehemiah's antagonists do seems like a logical choice, but God confuses their effort every time. Sanballat and the guys become comical in retrospect, but I can assure you, they were no joke to Nehemiah. They wanted to stop him at all costs, and they had no regard for his plans. The haters do not mince words, and they accuse Nehemiah of treason.

Nehemiah is ever faithful and full of resolve, and he doesn't give them an inch with which to play: "So I answered them and said to them, 'The God of heaven will give us success; therefore we His servants will arise and build, but you have no portion, right or memorial in Jerusalem'" (Neh. 2:20, NASB). If Taylor Swift had been around, Nehemiah would have been singing her song "Shake It Off" (partly because it fits the scene, but also because it is REALLY hard to get it out of your head once you have heard it). I can hear Nehemiah now (probably in a deeper voice):

But I keep cruising
Can't stop, won't stop moving
It's like I got this music
In my mind
Saying, "It's gonna be alright."

'Cause the players gonna play, play, play, play, play
And the haters gonna hate, hate, hate, hate, hate
Baby, I'm just gonna shake, shake, shake, shake, shake

I shake it off, I shake it off
Heart-breakers gonna break, break, break, break, break
And the fakers gonna fake, fake, fake, fake, fake
Baby, I'm just gonna shake, shake, shake, shake, shake
I shake it off, I shake it off.[37]

Nehemiah just shook it off. He told the haters, you have no part of this, and we are servants of God and we will not be denied… and neither will God. (I am sorry for the Taylor Swift reference. It seemed like a bad idea, but I like the words. Sorry. Try to stop thinking about it. Try hard. Just shake those thoughts off. Shake 'em off! Shake 'em off…off…off. Sorry. Really.)

In the next chapter, we'll look at why having a plan is important.

CHAPTER 5

GET TO WORK

Several years ago, we were serving a church in middle Georgia…not Middle Earth…equidistant between Macon and Augusta. While my wife, Lindsey, our kids, and I were not from there, it was certainly more of a home than anywhere else we had ever served. We loved that church and the community, but there was a problem.

The church had been around for a hundred years, but the current sanctuary had been rebuilt because of a lightning strike in the 1930s. Over seven decades, the church simply sprawled over a city block. They acquired property and houses, and they expanded to accommodate their growing church. The problem was there was no plan—no developed system to guide the church growth or pull it all together once they completed their facility needs.

Our family moved there with small children—a seven-week-old and a 21-month-old. You could not get around the campus without being outside, and the nursery was as far away from the sanctuary as you could be on the campus. This was not a comfort to parents of small children, even if they were the pastoral family who were required by God's law to love the church without reason or logic. Not really, but the pastoral family is supposed to hide their distaste. To exacerbate the sprawl issues, you could get to the sanctuary for worship five different ways. Yes, you read that correctly: FIVE different ways. There was no place to congregate before or after a church service, and the church members were feeling disconnected.

After I was hit by the car I realized another challenge first-hand. I found out you could not get from your car to the sanctuary without being exposed to the elements. During my recovery, I started off in a wheelchair for a while, then I moved to crutches and then to a cane. I was able to see through the eyes of many elderly and physically challenged people who require some assistance when moving about. In the event of a downpour, you just don't get to go to church that day. This was not good enough.

The church knew they had issues with their facilities, but they had been unable to solve them. Ten years before we arrived, they came close to addressing the issues with an exploratory process that produced recommendations and the option of a new building, but the church leadership decided to wait until later. In the Methodist Church world that is code for *we don't really want to lock in the current pastor for a long building project and we'd rather wait.* So, the problem just got worse.

When we arrived, it became clear the church needed to do something. The people were interested, and God was giving me and some leaders a vision. I and a church leader could actually see the new building that could tie everything together. A renovation/building process would pull all of the other buildings into a design that connected all of the spaces and established a flow pattern that would bring people together physically and spiritually on a Sunday for worship and at other times for activities. With a vision, we had work to do.

What emerged from hours upon hours of planning and discussing and developing was a plan that came to be called "Arise: United We Build" with due credit given to Nehemiah, of course. We prayed a great deal about discerning God's vision for us and attempting to understand what was the basis for serving God's vision.

During my time serving as an officer in the U.S. Navy, I deployed to southern Spain for seven months. Our unit worked 6 days per week from 6a – 6p, including physical training (PT) before the work day began. We did not have a lot of free time. When we did have the occasional two or three days off, we would travel, and I went on maybe three trips in seven months.

On one such trip, we went to Gibraltar, which I had only seen on insurance advertisements. It looks the same in person, by the way, only bigger...much bigger. The Romans believed that during Hercules' Twelve Labors, he came to that part of the world. There was a mountain that used to be the Titan Atlas that connected the two continents, and he smashed his way through connecting the Mediterranean Sea with the Atlantic Ocean. The Pillars of Hercules in Gibraltar and Morocco mark the spot where Hercules blasted through the western end of the world of antiquity. In mythology, the pillars marked the end of the world with Hades on the other side, and they served as warnings not to leave the Mediterranean Sea.

There are actual pillars, and we stood in Gibraltar at one site, looking across the strait to Africa, which appears so close. Many people were deterred from entering the Atlantic by that story. We all have our own Pillars of Hercules. They are barriers that restrict us and then define us. The exit of a body of water was blocked by an invisible wall that stretched from Europe to Africa. When we erect these pillars or allow them to be put in our way, we cannot fulfill our calling.

We know what those pillars can look like: I cannot free up time in the morning for prayer/devotional; how could I volunteer an hour per week; tithing would hamper my vacation and shopping budget; we can't pledge what we need to for church campaigns because it will stretch us too much; and it is too late for God to do something new in our lives. Our church building campaign was about pushing past barriers through the strength of God and our faith.

Paul tells us in Romans 4:16-25 that faith can look crazy at times. Abraham, the father of the Jewish people was given a promise by God that he would father a great nation as vast and impressive as the stars in the heaven as we stare up on a clear night. Paul uses Abraham as the example of faith because his circumstances were bleak. How in the world could Abraham have faith in God's plan as each day went by and with each birthday that passed? Abraham must have started to give up inside…little by little…the promise became less true and clear.

In contrast to that presumption, Paul says, "[H]e did not waiver in unbelief but grew strong in faith, giving glory to God and being fully assured that what God had promised, He was able to perform" (Rom. 4:19-20, NASB). Abraham's faith became his legacy and something we need to appreciate and emulate. God does amazing things, and He kept His word to Abraham.

God is in the *amazing* business! Back to our building campaign. We hired an expert to help us raise the necessary funds. Our expert has worked with some of the biggest churches and pastors in the country: Bill Hybels, John Ortberg, and Tim Keller, to name a few. At one of our early meetings with our fundraising consultant, either to deter us from our project or to wake us up, he told us if a church our size could raise our goal amount of $5M, "It would be amazing." That got my attention. Trusting in God for direction and provision, it sounded like a challenge to me and the others, and we were not deterred; we were resolved.

As Abraham aged and it got less likely that he and his elderly wife would have a child, he trusted even more…Abraham believed more resolutely. Paul says, Abraham was "as good as dead." Like the church member who told me I was serving "a dying church" or that friend who says losing weight isn't worth the effort, it is easy to believe we are "as good as dead." When he was nearly 100 years old, a baby came. The world may be telling you it is too late, that we are as good as dead. DO NOT believe the lie. The Devil may be whispering that lie in your ears right now as you read this book. Take heart! He did the same thing to Abraham. His belief/faith made him righteous in God's eyes, and God kept His promise. We are not "as good as dead," and you have a great thing to do right now in your life, and the results will be amazing!

Sometimes God gets our attention. When we are spread thin, and we are tested, we could falter. Yes, we could believe we are as good as dead, and we could lose heart/faith and give up. Don't. It is in those times that our faith can blossom and flourish; we will be amazed.

Faith is called to be put to work from time to time. Sure, it is great to trust in God and find assurance in the grace and salvation of Jesus. We believe when we cannot see. Faith is also tangible when we put ourselves to the work of God, trusting that even though we may not know the way or the means, we know God is in charge and leading us on our journey to accomplish His plans.

God's vision will be realized. May we be like Nehemiah and live as **a part** of God's vision and not **apart** from God's vision.

I find it amazing that Nehemiah didn't mess around. Nehemiah had never been to Jerusalem in his life. He lived in a palace, and he never had to worry about a thing except keeping the king happy and *un*-poisoned. This is like a barista from Starbucks in Beverly Hills, California, whose parents were from Georgia. He decides to go to the little small town, county seat where he grew up. The Californian barista shows up one day, and then the next day he is rebuilding their old county courthouse that was hit by lightning and burned to charred brick remains 50 years earlier.

Imagine the responses. Depending on the part of the state, he might have been shot just for being from California. As Chevy Chase said in "Fletch Lives" when questioned in Louisiana about his *Yankiness*, "I'm not really anything, I'm from California." The sly southern barrister responds, "You said it, mister." So assuming the Californian barista doesn't get shot, he certainly would have had his sanity questioned. He has a connection to the job that needs to be done through his family, but he doesn't have any obvious responsibility or accountability. Like that hostile environment, Nehemiah has a job to do even in the midst of ridicule and physical threats: he gets to work.

Where does he begin? Nehemiah begins in the most obvious place: the gate…the **Sheep Gate** to be precise. The high priest and his fellow priests hung the doors to the gate, and then the men of Jericho and Zaccur worked on the walls that connected the gate to the **Tower of the Hundred** and the **Tower of Hananel**.

> Then Eliashib the high priest arose with his
> brothers the priests and built the Sheep Gate; they

consecrated it and hung its doors. They consecrated the wall to the Tower of the Hundred and
the Tower of Hananel. Next to him the men of
Jericho built, and next to them Zaccur the son of
Imri built. (Neh. 3:1-2, NASB)

The gate allowed access to the city, and the towers enabled the wall watchers to view who comes to the gate or approaches the walls. The wall was beginning to take shape, and Nehemiah was coordinating the effort with anyone who made themselves available.

All parts of a wall are essential. A gate without a wall is nothing. An imposing wall without a gate to control access is just a barrier to be walked around. Towers are needed to anchor the wall as it changes direction and follows the boundary of the city. All three parts are needed to build a wall that keeps people out but also allows controlled access to what is inside the city. Nehemiah was off to a good start, but there was much more to do.

Throughout the rest of Nehemiah 3, we see the work that the crew did. They worked on this section, and then that one. They built a wall until they reached a gate, and then, "they laid its beams and hung its doors with its bolts and its bars" (Neh. 3:3, NASB). Nehemiah and his team didn't try to reinvent the wheel, and he used anyone he could find: goldsmiths, priests, temple servants, city folk, country folk—men of the valley OR *valley boys*, family members—including sons and daughters, … They were methodical, and they paid attention to the work at hand. Nehemiah was attentive to everything that had to happen, and he was thankful for every single person who came out to work. Here is a diagram that shows the work as I describe it in this section. Nehemiah recorded every section of the construction project and the people who did the work.

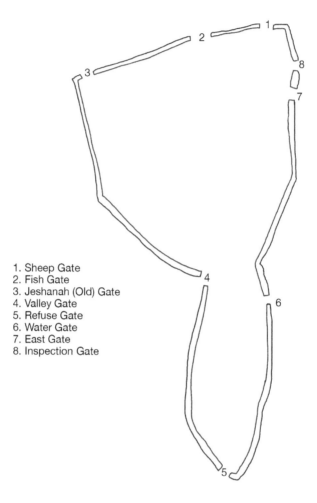

1. Sheep Gate
2. Fish Gate
3. Jeshanah (Old) Gate
4. Valley Gate
5. Refuse Gate
6. Water Gate
7. East Gate
8. Inspection Gate

The construction project moved to the **Fish Gate**, Hassenaah and his brothers hung its doors and installed the bolts and bars. Meremoth worked alongside Meshullum, Zadok, and the men of Tekoa. Nehemiah sends us a message about the people of Tekoa, a town 10 miles south of Jerusalem. They are geographically close to Jerusalem, but as a city, they were divided. Nehemiah tells us the common people honored God and their leadership did not. Their nobles would not work with him, and refused to lift a finger in support of God's good work (Neh. 3:5, NASB). They probably feared a resurgence of Jerusalem would lessen their control of the people of Tekoa…more haters at work.

Joaida and Meshullum, assisted by Melatieh leading the men of Gibeon, and Jadon leading the men of Mizpah, repaired the **Jeshanah Gate**, hanging the doors, installing the bolts and bars. Nehemiah put anyone willing and able to work. The next section of the wall was led by Uzziel from the goldsmiths' guild and Hananiah, a perfumer. They worked on the wall all the way to the section widened in preparation of the siege by the Assyrians called the **Broad Wall**.

The work continued, led by Rephaiah, the mayor of half of Jerusalem—the city was divided into two districts. Part of the wall was composed of private homes, and Jedaiah rebuilt his house, improving the integrity of the wall, while Hattush worked next to him. Malkijah and Hasshub rebuilt the next section, including the **Tower of Furnaces**. Alongside their team, Shallum, the mayor of the other half of Jerusalem, worked with his team. He was so dedicated to this project that he brought his daughters out to work the wall as well.

For any of us who have ever needed a workout buddy, this is a lesson to us. I cannot tell you how many times I have been more dedicated to a workout when my wife joined in. When I join her or she joins me for a digital on-demand workout, it is always easier to have her by my side. We encourage each other. All of us could use someone else to encourage or motivate us. At the very least, misery loves company, and someone jumping in can be comforting.

Shallum would have been under serious public scrutiny from the other leaders, including Sanballat and his toadies. Shallum was so committed to God's plan and Nehemiah's vision, he brought his daughters to join him. He exposed his beloved daughters to ridicule and potential physical harm to teach them about honoring and serving God. This was a very public display of devotion to God and an affirmation to what Nehemiah and the construction team were doing.

This dedicated work continued on the wall as Hanun and the villagers of Zanaoh were especially prolific in their zeal and productivity. We all know overachievers, and the people from Zanoah set the bar really high. Nehemiah records just how successful they were in their work. They rebuilt the **Valley Gate** and they repaired 1,500 feet of the wall, all the way to the **Refuse Gate**. That gate was completed by Malkajah, who was also a mayor but of Beth Hakkeram, which was located right outside Jerusalem. A very clear divide was emerging, not that leaders were taking sides for political reason, but they were choosing God over political expediency and position and governing power.

Not only were the men of Mizpah engaged in the project, their mayor, Shallun, led the work at the **Fountain Gate**, where they repaired and roofed the gate. They also rebuilt the wall of the **Pool of Siloam** at the **King's Garden** as far as the steps that go down from the old City of David. Next to their work, another mayor led the effort; Nehemiah, son of Azbuck, the mayor of half the district of Beth Zur. They worked in front of the **Tomb of David** as far as the **Pool** and the **House of Heroes**—the tombs of David's Might Men.

Politicians were not the only public figures laboring in support of God and Nehemiah. The Levites were led by Rehum, and they worked alongside Hashabiah, mayor of the half-district of Keilah. Hashabiah did not have much support from his district, but he was there in force working with Henadad, the mayor of the other Keilah half-district with men from that district.

The rebuilding work continued on the next section, which was in front of the **Ascent** to the **Armory** as far as the **Angle**, and the work was led by Mayor Jeshua of Mizpah's son Ezer (Neh. 3:19, NASB). Baruch, son of Zabbai, led the work done from the **Angle** to the door of the house of Eliashib, the high priest. Meremoth, son of Uriah and grandson of Hakkoz, was responsible for the work from Priest **Eliashib's Door** to the end of his house. The priests who lived in the high priest's neighborhood led the work on the wall from his house forward: Benjamin and Hasshub worked their section; and Azariah, son of Maaseiah and grandson of Ananiah, did the work by his house.

The teams worked in conjunction, connecting as the timing of the work allowed. From **Priest Azariah's house** to the **Angle** at the **Corner**, the wall was rebuilt by Binnui, son of Henadad. Palal, son of Uzai, led the work opposite the **Angle** and the tower, extending from the **Upper Palace of the king**, which was right near the **Court of the Guard**. Pedaiah, son of Parosh, led the work on the next section supported by the Temple staff who lived on the hill of Opheh. Their work went eastward from Palal's worksite to opposite the **Water Gate** and the palace tower. The men from Tekoa completed the section from that tower to the **Wall of Ophel**.

The work around the **Horse Gate** was done by residents. The priests who lived there worked above the gate, each working on the area in front of their home. There was a larger section in front of the house of Zadok, Immer's son, and Zadok led that work. The next section was under the supervision of Shecaniah's son Shemaiah. Shemaiah was the keeper of the **East Gate**. Next to Shecaniah was Hananiah, son of Shelemiah, and then Hanun, the sixth son of Zalaph. Meshullam, son of Berekiah, had a storage shed for his supplies, and he worked on the wall across from the shed. Malkijah the goldsmith led the team repairing the wall as far as the **House of the Temple Support Staff and Merchants**. They worked all the way to the **Inspection Gate** and onward to the **Upper Room at the Corner**. From there, the goldsmiths and merchants worked on the wall between that corner and the **Sheep Gate**.

Nehemiah didn't use cutting edge design or innovation. He started the work at the Sheep Gate, and they kept working until they walled the city back to the Sheep Gate. He put people to work repairing the portion of the wall near their home. This was smart, because people have a little more motivation to secure the wall by where they live. If the wall has a weak point, that is where an enemy will attack to gain access. Thus, if you do shoddy work on the wall by your house, be prepared to die first when the wall is tested. In short, everyone Nehemiah could convince to work, he put to work, and they worked with a purpose.

When we find ourselves in a state of disrepair—where our health is not where it should be—we can come up with a lengthy list of reasons we *can't* get better. It becomes about time, inconvenience, and physics: a body at rest stays at rest. If we can get that rocket off the launch pad, we can take flight. We do not have to reinvent the wheel: there are time-tested approaches to eating healthier, exercising, and making space for God to work on us.

We should use any means available to us. If we have resident experts at our disposal, ask for help. If you know a dietician or an athlete, ask for help. Speaking from experience, people like to talk about things they know about, and most people in your life like you and they will want to help you. Ask for help. DO something now—today!

In the next chapter, we will look at getting moving…and staying moving.

CHAPTER 6

DEFEAT RESISTANCE

Now it came about that when Sanballat heard that
we were rebuilding the wall, he became furious
and very angry and mocked the Jews. He spoke
in the presence of his brothers and the wealthy
men of Samaria and said, "What are these feeble
Jews doing? Are they going to restore it for themselves? Can they offer sacrifices? Can they finish
in a day? Can they revive the stones from the
dusty rubble even the burned ones?" Now Tobiah
the Ammonite was near him and he said, "Even
what they are building—if a fox should jump on
it, he would break their stone wall down!" (Neh.
4:1-3, NASB)

NEHEMIAH DID NOT WAIT for opposition; he went at the wall
with the intention to finish that great work. All of these teams
worked, and they worked hard…and fast. There is no reason to
wait to seize the initiative. I learned training with the U.S. Marines,
seizing the initiative is War Fighting 101. Nehemiah seized the
initiative, taking the high ground mentally and physically. They

were doing the work God called them to do, and God responds to our faithfulness.

God is always more faithful than we are. God saw their work and was ready for what came next. Sanballat…was…not…happy. That could be the understatement of the book of Nehemiah. Just like the Devil wants us lethargic and unhealthy, with our defenses against illness down, Sanballat wanted Jerusalem…and the people… vulnerable and controllable. Nehemiah's plan was working, and he knew he had to do something before it really was too late.

Sanballat is threatened. We know all we need to know about him by where he is from and the language he uses. He is a Samaritan and hyper-critical of the Jews. It bothers him that they would dare try to return things to the way they were before the kingdom collapsed—how God intended for them to be. Samaria was in the heart of Israel or the Northern Tribes, and they have disagreed with each other ever since King Solomon died and the Kingdom split into the Judah and Israel kingdoms. They disagreed about where to sacrifice to God, which is probably why Sanballat brought it up: *there go those Jews, still trying to offer sacrifices in Jerusalem and nowhere else.* Like a toady, Tobiah the Ammonite (Ammon: another long-time enemy of the Jews) makes that quip about a fox knocking down the wall if it landed on it. Hilarious!

Did I tell you, I love Nehemiah?! He prays to God to not let those dissenters off the hook, and then gets back to work. They restore the wall to half its height surrounding Jerusalem, "[F]or the people had a mind to work" (Neh. 4:6b, NASB). Now Sanballat and his ilk decide to kill Nehemiah and his workers, "Our enemies said, 'They will not know or see until we come among them, kill them and put a stop to the work'" (Neh. 4:11, NASB). Nehemiah knew he must be prepared or their mission would fail.

Sanballat was not a Jerusalem Jew, he was just ruling them. When he found out the wall was being rebuilt, he lost his mind. Sanballat ordered his henchman from Samaria and the soldiers under his control to assemble immediately. Of course, Sanballat had to spin things because the evidence of God's support was over-whelming. He did the only thing he could do: he downplayed how well they had actually done. He could not ignore the wall: it *was not* there one minute, and it *was* there the next.

We all have critics ready to denounce us, root against us, or just straight work to undo what we have done. Sanballat was no different from any jealous person we come across. They do not care to know how much time you have put into bettering yourself, they will discount it to suit their needs. This approach prevents them from thinking about their own struggles and failures. It is always infinitely easier to criticize someone else than putting the needed effort into improving their own lives. Jealousy blinds people to a future they can help shape and form.

Sanballat could have tried to develop the people around him, but he chose the simpler route of pushing them down rather than building them up. He responded to their progress by saying, they may have a wall but it is built with *bubblegum and shoestrings*. Okay, he did not say that, but he did say it was like Swiss cheese and was really no barrier at all.

Sanballat's toady, Tobiah the Ammonite, chimed in with his two cents supporting Sanballat. Shocker! It reminds me of the Looney Tunes cartoon with Spike the big, tough bulldog, and Chester, his diminutive sidekick. Chester bounces around Spike agreeing to whatever he wants to do and fawning all over him as if he were the best thing since sliced bread. That was Tobiah the toady. *Yeah, Sanballat, that ain't no wall! Yeah, I bet if the wind blew hard enough it would fall right over. If a fox ran around the city on their new wall it would collapse in a heap as soon as his hind legs left each brick.* Consider the source.

It did not take long before word got back to Nehemiah that Sanballat was using his spin machine to undercut their work on the wall and was plotting against him. God made sure Nehemiah knew of the tightened state, and Nehemiah responded by going back to God in prayer, asking for His intervention. Nehemiah asked for God to stop Sanballat and his threat. He did not just ask for Sanaballat to fail; he asked for Sanballat and his allies to be destroyed. Nehemiah told God they insulted God's builders, and they should never be forgiven. Punishment must be swift and final (Neh. 4:4-5, NASB).

Nehemiah asked for God to intervene. He asked God to return their behavior right back at them, calling for a foreign enemy to scheme, plot, and overtake them. Nehemiah wanted their own planning to be replicated by a foreign enemy and used against Sanballat and his henchmen. There was no confusion about what must happen: God needed to show up and definitively declare who would win this battle.

With complete confidence in God's plan, Nehemiah set his face toward the goal of finishing the wall...*he set his face like flint.* Nehemiah would have known Isaiah's prophecies. In the second part of what we know as the book of Isaiah, Eugene Peterson calls "Messages of Comfort," there is a message Nehemiah must have told himself again and again—every night when he dared close his eyes and every morning when he sprang to alert to begin the day's tasks.

Isaiah promises a Servant of God will come, and He will do what needs to be done. Isaiah delivered these empowering words,

"I gave my back to those who beat Me, and My cheeks to those who tore out My beard. I did not hide My face from scorn and spitting. The Lord God will help Me; therefore I have not been humiliated; therefore I have set My face like flint, and I know I will not be put to shame" (Isa. 50:6-7, HCSB). Isaiah comforts with words of power and victory in the face of certain defeat.

Followers of Jesus believe Isaiah was talking about Jesus—our suffering Savior. Isaiah describes the torture and abuse Jesus suffered, while providing hope and strength. These words of promise do more than just convey determination in the midst of suffering. Isaiah's words provide the imagery we need to commit to needed change in our own lives.

Isaiah's Suffering Servant *sets His face like flint*. Flint is found in sedimentary rock formations. Oddly enough, flint is found in small nodules in sedimentary rock like chalk or limestone.[38] Chalk is soft, while flint is very hard. It was valuable for making tools and weapons and starting fires as far back as the Stone Age. Flint was strong, and it was essential.

Isaiah tells us when we want to get something accomplished, we have to mean it. We do not set our face like chalk; we set our face like flint. Our plans are *set in stone*. When we *set our faces like flint*, we will not take no for an answer. We will either complete the task God has given us or we will die trying.

Nehemiah received his mission from God, and with God's help, he had inspired them to work…and work…and stay determined. They connected all of the sections of the wall. The work was progressing, and the wall was now half of the planned height. There was no way Sanballat could ignore this achievement, no matter what he thought of their craftsmanship.

The wall was solid. It was formidable, and everyone who saw it—Jew and non-Jew alike—recognized what it meant. It was as if a vessel to an important organ was being restored. The essence and life was returning to Jerusalem. Like oxygen-laden blood supplying the circulatory and respiratory systems of the body, Jerusalem began to take on some semblance of what it was. Sanballat had to act even as God was working out His plan.

Sanballat gathered his panel of miscreants to develop a plan to destroy Nehemiah and his efforts. Tobiah was never too far away from him. He grabbed the leaders from the Arabs, the Ammonites, and Ashdodites. They conspired to not only stop Nehemiah and the workers, but they strived to take the wall down brick by brick.

God kept Nehemiah privy to their devious plans. Sanballat showed up at this bike race with an old-school Schwinn bicycle, and God was riding a carbon-fiber frame with the latest and lightest components. Sanballat did not stand a chance, but he was blinded by greed and anger. Nehemiah reinforced their efforts with prayer…constant prayer…life-giving prayer…breathing in and breathing out prayer that sustains the soul and mind as well as the body.

Nehemiah implemented his own version of the expression *praise the Lord and pass the ammunition.* They prayed without ceasing *and* set a sentry rotation that operated 24 hours per day. Whether the citizens were working, sleeping, or playing, the workers were armed and ready to defend their work. They were not just protecting the construction site, they were fighting for God Himself.

Upon hearing from his supporters that they would attack at night or while they were working on the wall, Nehemiah announced his plan to thwart them. "[T]hen I stationed men in the lowest parts of the space behind the wall, the exposed places, and I stationed the people in families with their swords, spears and bows. When I saw their fear, I rose and spoke to the nobles, the officials and the rest of the people: 'Do not be afraid of them; remember the Lord who is great and awesome, and fight for your brothers, your sons, your daughters, your wives and your houses'" (Neh. 4:13-14, NASB). Amen! Remember the Lord who is great and awesome…and fight! (Yes, sir! Tell me which position you want me to take and give me a weapon as I go!)

From then on, Nehemiah had the people ready to fight while they worked: one group worked as the other stood watch. When someone had to carry a load of bricks or supplies, they carried the load with one hand while they held onto a spear or sword with the other hand. The builders worked with both hands, but they each had a sword in a sheath on their hip.

Nehemiah had a trumpeter nearby who would signal if there was an attack because they were spread all over the wall doing their work. "At whatever place you hear the sound of the trumpet, rally to us there. Our God will fight for us" (Neh. 4:20, NASB). Nehemiah convinced them to not leave Jerusalem to return to their homes outside the wall, and they slept in their clothes at the work site with one hand on a weapon around the clock. Sleep deprived and exhausted, they worked tirelessly to complete their work. "So neither I, my brothers, my servants, nor the men of the guard who followed me, none of us removed our clothes, each *took* his weapon *even to* the water" (Neh. 4:23, NASB). This was certainly a slower way to work, but this is what they had to do to ensure they could live to do God's work.

That is what health is all about: living in such a way to praise, worship, and serve God longer. The way we take care of our bodies has a great deal of influence on how long we get to live in this life. (I know this is obvious, but sometimes the most important principles in life are simple—like say, God is love.) The hard part is connecting our longevity with *how* we live each day we are given. We are not alone: *Our God will fight for us.*

In the days after I returned home from the hospital, pain was the dominant feeling. Whether it was in the morning, the afternoon, the evening, or during the middle of the night, something was hurting. My ankle needed two weeks to recover from the trauma before the surgeon would operate and rebuild my ankle. That meant the splint I was wearing, covering my left leg from my hip to my toes would have ample time to completely eliminate my quadriceps muscle. You never think about the fact that if your leg is straight all of the time and you are lying on your back 24 hours a day, that muscle isn't used and therefore dies. I know now.

The first morning I awoke at 2 am as I did for months to follow, unable to sleep. I learned to get out of bed so my wife could sleep, and moved myself on crutches to the living room. Our furniture was not sufficient for my needs, so that borrowed hospital bed came in very handy over the next six weeks. We are forever grateful to our pharmacist friend, because that bed was a lifesaver. I would toss and turn or watch television until around 5 am, when I would fade back to sleep for another hour and a half.

That first morning, I went to God for help in my normal devotion time. After a prayer, I pulled out my *Faith Sharing New Testament*, and opened it to the Psalms. I could not read the words. This was a time when I needed to read a word from David, as a lamentation or to find some encouragement from a guy who knew the full range of emotions. He knew the heights of a coronation and battlefield victories, and the lows of the loss of a child or embracing the gravity of his sin. I needed to read his words. I could not.

It took a while—7-10 days—before I was able to read again. Because of the concussion I suffered by cracking the driver's windshield with the back of my head, I had done some damage to the back of my brain—the area where our eyes process things. I could not focus on the words. The television and other screens all had halos around them. I COULD NOT READ! It was very scary and unnerving. But I could pray, and I did.

I needed God's help now more than ever. God was ever faithful. I knew that I could not do this on my own, but I didn't have to do it on my own. I began to rebuild the wall—my body.

I knew, deep down, that my God was fighting for me. Every day, I worked with one hand on the bricks loaded up on my back, and my other hand was on my weapon. I focused on one day at a time. I never looked beyond that morning, or the afternoon, or making it through another night. Even though I didn't have a hunger to eat, I knew enough from my experience as a pastor visiting sick people, I needed to eat…so, I did. I ate three meals a day whether I wanted to or not.

God was fighting for me. I was dealing with the pain. I tried to get off my pain medication as soon as I could. Because of my injuries, I had to have an injection of blood thinners every night for six weeks to ward off blood clots. Every night my wife would inject my stomach with this painful syringe of medicine. I would dread it at times. I joked that this was how my wife was able to vent some of her frustration at me for my failings as a patient, but she always denied it.

This was our routine. I would crutch around the house to go to the hospital bed and the bathroom, and that was about it. Breakfast would come, then lunch, then dinner, then my injection, and then the day would end going to bed with my leg elevated on pillows. In between, my wounds from the road rash had to be dressed as my hand, elbow, left hip, and backside were all inured in the accident. It sounds bad, I know; it reads bad as I type it, but the injuries didn't define me. God did.

In the mundane of every day, God was working. My road rash was healing. My brain was healing: I could read again and the halos were gone. My fractured vertebra was healing. The inflammation in my sacroiliac joint was getting more tolerable (even though to date, I still cannot sit without discomfort). My rebuilt ankle was healing as the skin was healing and the plates and screws were anchoring new bone growth and strengthening. *My God was fighting!*

The rebuilding was beginning, but now I needed more than wounds to heal. I had to begin the process of rehabilitation. My back and core had to be re-strengthened, and I had to learn to walk again. For many of us, this is where we find ourselves even today. We are ready for a change, but now we have to do something.

Before I could begin my rehab program because of my back, I would sneak outside to get some sunshine and crutch up the street as my *workout*. I am someone who works out five days a week. Going from that to lying on my back for six weeks was not easy. I had to have some outlet.

When I was finally cleared for rehab, I started off with three visits a week. The first goal was to work on my core strength. Then it was to go from two crutches to one crutch to no crutches. I wish I could tell you God made it all go swimmingly and that it was easy, but it was not. It was hard—one of the hardest things I have ever done in my life. That is what rebuilding is like: it's hard. But that *good work* needs to be done!

If you are at this point in your life, where you are finally tired of not being healthy, it is time to act…right now. Don't wait. Our God is ready to fight for us. God wants us to be healthier; God created us for that. Sin, sickness and death are not God's creations, and they were not meant for us. We have to deal with them in this life. Now is the day to deal with them.

Begin with a goal. Any goal will do as long as it helps you get closer to what God intends for you and your body, mind and soul. If you are in a bad place spiritually, find a discipline that strengthens that part of your life. Add devotional time with God, Scripture reading, prayer time, volunteer, do mission work, or get a support group who will hold you accountable. Do all of those. Do some of them. Do at least ONE of them.

You have to remove a part of your life to make room for this new discipline; make sure it is something that needs to go. Don't stop talking to your mother to add time for God. Don't neglect your friends, spouse, children, or your job to make the time. I will just about guarantee you there are minutes in your day on Facebook, Twitter, Instagram, Snapchat, or spent using the Devil's main tools—the Internet or the television.

The same works for exercise. If you need to lose some weight or you are too sedentary, get out of the house and get at it. Trade 30 minutes of sitting for 30 minutes of walking, running, swimming, bike riding, or using an exercise machine. Once you clear it with your doctor, get into an exercise program.

Our God will fight for us. God will respond to your movement. Even if it is something as simple as wanting to become more well-read or more proficient at your job or smarter, and you make strides in that direction, God will respond to you. You will get stronger and healthier.

I love historical fiction, books, and movies: there is a realness there with which I connect. I enjoyed a great movie about the American revolution called *The Patriot*. Mel Gibson stars as a South Carolina farmer who was also a colonel in the colonial army, fighting for the British in regional skirmishes and battles. His character is loosely based on Francis Marion —the Swamp Fox, and he points out before the war, as he lobbies against it, that this war would not be far off in the wilderness but very near. It would be fought around their homes and in their towns.

He doesn't want to fight, having seen enough of it, but he is drawn into the war. He has trained his sons to shoot for hunting. They are good marksmen—they are able and accurate. As they prepare to engage the British, he reminds them of his sage wisdom: "Aim small, miss small." Simple, but SO true.[39]

Nehemiah and his workers saw results. The wall started to go up. Connections to other areas were happening. It actually looked like a wall. God was fighting for them, and they were getting stronger. Bit by bit…incrementally, things were happening.

We need goals. Getting healthier is not a goal—that's a theme or idea. A goal only exists as such if you are working towards it. If we aren't, then it is just a dream. Goals are getting healthier by eliminating dessert or eating two apples a day or eating salad every night or not eating food after 9p.m. or going to bed by 10p.m. or running a 5k race or a marathon or learning to swim or completing a triathlon. Those are goals. And there are manageable goals as well as bold and amazing and bodacious goals. They all need God to make them happen—to come to fruition.

Sanballat was shrewd, and, like countless generals and politicians who followed him throughout history, propaganda was his weapon of choice. The word was pushed down to the residents in and around Jerusalem. In spite of the results, the people were buying the lies: the workers are exhausted; the trash is piling up higher than the walls; and even if the whole city shows up to work, it CANNOT be done.

It happens…to the best of us. When we are working as hard as we think we can work, doubt starts to creep in. Maybe when you stop losing weight on your *new* plan or you have not been able to maintain your gym schedule because of work or family, and you start to struggle to see the fruit of your hard work, all it takes is the wrong comment. It could be from a friend who makes a misguided statement about your clothes seeming tighter or asking *why* you stopped trying to lose weight when you haven't. We have a choice: we can either give in to their comment and give up, or we can put our foot in the ground and fight back. The people of Jerusalem heard one too many comments, and they, too, had a choice.

The people started to believe they would not ever complete the task. They worked hard, but the negativity was taking hold. The people started to give up. They lost hope. They lost sight of Nehemiah's vision. So what did Nehemiah do? Nehemiah needed to act.

Sanballat's plan was to actually attack the builders, no longer with words but with swords. They pushed their message with an all-out propaganda offensive to weaken the knees of the builders before they even saw one of their troops coming. The battle would be over before it was fought.

The builders started to see ghosts that were not there. The New York Jets allowed the NFL to mic up their quarterback for a big game with the New England Patriots. Coming off a win, quarterback Sam Darnold was looking like a good quarterback. He was gaining confidence, and so was his team. Then, the Patriots happened: they sacked him several times and intercepted four of his passes. It seemed to Darnold like the Patriots defense was all over the field. At one point on the sideline, ESPN went live with his mic as he told his coach: "I'm seeing ghosts out there." The world stopped, or at least it seemed like it. Darnold just admitted that he was so rattled by the Patriots defense he was seeing players that weren't there. Commentators, ex-players, and players in the game alike knew that was a bad statement. Even if it was true, you cannot ever say that out loud. That game was over for Darnold and the Jets.

The builders were having a *Sam Darnold moment*. Without the necessary forces to even complete the task, the builders were convinced their enemies had them surrounded. Nehemiah was praying around the clock, but he had to act now. The same truth that hits us when we struggle or get off track had to be realized for the builders. Nehemiah had to recast the vision.

Nehemiah assessed the threat. He knew where the wall had natural defenses because of topography. He also knew that even though the wall was ahead of schedule, there were spots where the wall was vulnerable. It was in those sections of the wall that he placed armed guards to defend the city and the other builders. Nehemiah prepared a rotation for the guards, placing people with their family members—the people they trusted absolutely. There would be no room for doubt. They were armed with swords, lances, and bows. With the people in place, Nehemiah took a long, slow walk to check the security of the wall for himself. He also showed their enemies, that he knew exactly what they did and did not have accomplished. It was a very public display of authority and initiative for what work was going to be completed.

After his inspection, Nehemiah gathered everybody in the city. He sent messengers to summon the nobles and officials.

He sent out loud, town crier-types to announce a meeting of everyone in Jerusalem. As they all gathered together, Nehemiah set them straight.

Nehemiah reminded them of how far they had come and at a record pace. He took none of the credit, and he told them to think about God. Nehemiah said put your minds not on the enemy, not on the work still to be done, and not on the Babylonians who took your families away and destroyed the temple and the city. He told them to put their thoughts on God and His faithfulness.

We deal with the same distraction and flaws in our faith. But the Apostle Peter echoes the same message of Nehemiah: cast your cares on God (1 Pet. 5:7, NASB). Take every concern and shred of doubt and transfer it onto God. Go to the bank of doubt, make a withdrawal and transfer it to God's account. He can handle it; God knows what to do with our challenges.

Nehemiah said take all of your fear and doubt and give it to God; then, fight. Our God is mighty and strong—"great and awesome"—and we will not be defeated. You are not fighting for yourselves; you can have second thoughts. No, the people were to fight for their brothers, their sons and daughters, and their wives, and they were to defend their homes. God is ready to act, but were they?

The people were ready, and they looked like it. They were so prepared, they intimidated Sanballat and his henchmen. God took the want-to out of their stomachs, and the builders went back to work. With the immediate threat under control, Nehemiah established a new plan. The builders would no longer be able to focus solely on construction, because they now had to be ready to fight.

When I served in the Navy, both on active duty as a Supply officer and in the Reserves as a chaplain, I had the honor of serving with the Seabees. The name *Seabees* comes from the acronym for their unit description: Construction Battalion—CB. They are the construction force of the U.S. Navy with civil engineering officers in their leadership. Seabees are equipment operators, plumbers, electricians, and builders. They are trained by the Marines and follow them into combat once an area is secured. They build infrastructure and rebuild communities. They have a special mission. Their motto is "We Build. We Fight."

Nehemiah's builders were the first Seabees, and they were good at what they did. His new plan was to rotate the builders through building shifts and defense shifts. He equipped the builders with armor as well as their weapons to repel an assault. The common laborers had a tool in one hand and a spear nearby. The master builders kept a sword strapped to their hip as they led the work on different sections of the wall.

Nehemiah oversaw the whole operation, staying on the move, forever vigilant. In the event of an attack, he kept a trumpeter near him, so he could sound the alarm to defeat their enemies. He told the builders, the officials, and the residents to listen for the trumpet. If they ever heard it—morning, noon, afternoon, or night—they were expected to come running, armed for combat. Nehemiah told them, you better come running, because God will be there ahead of you, waiting on you to join the fray.

And so it continued. Nehemiah ordered everyone to stay inside the city limits of the wall. There would be no more going out or coming in through the gates for now. They worked from first light until the last bit of sunlight leaked from the horizon. People worked on the wall and were prepared for battle. When they were not building, they were on the security detail. They built. They were ready to fight.

From Nehemiah, as the head of the construction project, to the supervisors, and all the way down to the guy who carried the mortar, they worked. All of them worked through the heat of the day and slept in their work clothes at night; ready to start back as soon as the first hint of light broke through the darkness of the sky. They were so prepared, they carried a spear when they went to the bathroom or to get a drink of water. They were vigilant.

There will be naysayers. There always are. We have our own Sanballats and Tobiahs running around our towns, in our homes, schools, offices, and churches. They CANNOT be allowed to deter us from God's purposes for us. We must make a stand!

In the adaptation of J.R.R. Tolkien's "Lord of the Rings" trilogy, there is a powerful scene in the first movie, "The Fellowship of the Ring." The fellowship is beginning to realize how dire the circumstance is on their quest to destroy the ring of Mordor. (If you have no idea what I am talking about, I will pray for you. You really need to see the movies, read the book, or, ideally, do both. There are great lessons about the light and the darkness that apply to our faith. Seriously, check it out!) They are running for their lives and fighting against the demon spawn orcs, and they are grossly outnumbered.

There are nine in the fellowship: a wizard, two men, one elf, one dwarf, and four Hobbits. Our heroes manage to near the escape of the cavernous underground kingdom in the Mines of Moria when a demon balgor called Durin's Bane shows up. Gandolf, the all-knowing wizard, sends the rest of the fellowship to the stairs escaping to the outside while he stays to battle the towering demon. They watch fearfully and awestruck, hoping he will join them in their escape.

Gandolf makes his stand in the middle of the bridge of Khazad-dum with nothing but seemingly endless expanse below him. As the demon approaches, Gandolf declares, "You cannot pass. I am a servant of the secret fire, wielder of the flame of Arnor. The dark fire will not avail you; flame of Udun!" they battle it out on the bridge, and he says, "Go back to the shadow." The battle continues, and Gandolf makes his stand and shouts, "You shall not pass!" He slams his staff into the rock, breaking the bridge and the enormous demon steps forward and the bridge falls apart, and it crashes to its death. As it falls, it pulls Gandolf down as well using its whip to pull his leg over the side. Gandolf is later transformed and returns in a perfect state, ensuring the triumph of the fellowship.[40]

It was a heck of a thing when Gandolf died…a heck of a thing. Moving on. We have to get to the point on our journey when we are on the bridge of Khazad-dum, and we make a stand: "I am a follower of Jesus, and no demon or temptation or fleshly desire is going to keep me from God's purpose for me." We must decide to make our stand: "I shall not be defeated by this!" "You shall not pass!"

In the next chapter, we will look at what it takes to make lasting change…committed to our purpose…like Gandolf!

CHAPTER 7

MAKE A LASTING CHANGE

THE MACHINE WAS HUMMING along nicely: people were working hard, their enemies were paralyzed in cowardice, and progress was being made. So, our lives go as well. You know as well as I do what happens next—something unforeseen slowed the work. Unrest. Lots and lots of unrest. In fact, protestors filled the streets. This time, the problem was not from without but within.

Jews were protesting Jews! Brothers and sisters had enough, not from the Babylonians, but from other members of God's chosen race. The Enemy uses all sorts of means to delay God's work and God's people. They did not protest having to work on the wall or having to serve the king of Babylon. No, they were crying out to God because *Jews* were violating God's law once again.

Nehemiah tells us husbands and wives—everyone—came out to protest their own countrymen. God told His people they could be bond-servants, signing on for a designated term to serve a fellow Jew. In the year of Jubilee—every 50 years—terms of bond-service and land deals were ended. Property—people and land—were returned to their owners—servants became autonomous again and land reverted to the original tribal owner. Most importantly, God said Jews were not to be treated as slaves but as hired hands. When Jubilee came, the bond-servants were given their freedom back. No one should be forced to become a slave for life. At least, that was what God's law said (Lev. 25:39-40, NASB).

Nehemiah met with the nobles and officials—the very ones working with him on the wall—and proceeded to dress them down…chew them out…give them a piece of his mind…whatever works for you so you understand Nehemiah was upset. He had worked too hard to restore God's people to have to go backwards. However, we do need to go back in the story just a bit.

When Nehemiah returned from Babylon, he began butting heads with Sanballat and his fellow corrupt landowners and politicians. He saw very quickly that they had slaves…Jewish slaves… working for them. They were poor and could not provide for themselves. They sold them to these foreigners to survive. Nehemiah saw it, and he was enraged.

If you have ever been involved with fundraising for a charity or a cause, you understand how hard it can be. Lindsey and I have married friends who serve as volunteers for the Juvenile Diabetes Research Foundation (JDRF), Georgia Chapter. This year, they are serving as the coordinators for the annual fundraiser gala. It is the largest fundraising event in Atlanta…bigger than any charity event in the area. This is an area with more than 4.6 million people. Over the years, the gala has raised over $30M for JDRF. Our friends are in charge of the gala in 2020—the 25th anniversary.

Our friends know what Nehemiah learned, it is hard to raise money. Nehemiah did not have to raise $30M, but he did have to raise the money to buy back his Jewish brothers and sisters. They were so in debt, they were working it off. They did whatever they were told to do with fear of imprisonment, or even death, if they did not. Nehemiah raised the required money to buy not one or two, but all of them out of bondage. That is why he was so angry at the scene of this protest.

Nehemiah addressed his fellow Jewish leaders, *we worked hard…really hard…to pay back those debts, and now you have taken the place of the foreigners. Now, YOU have become the landowners and slave-owners.* He said, Shame on you! The foreigners do not serve God, and Nehemiah suggested they do not know any better, but the Jews certainly do. He wondered aloud if it was time for another gala. Was it time for another fundraiser?! The protestors had mortgaged their homes and fields to pay their debts, but that was not enough. Now, they were having to sell themselves and their children, and that was not right or part of God's plan. Nehemiah had to stop the injustice and corruption of God's law.

Men of power and authority are not usually short on ideas or words, but these men—nobles and officials all—were silent. They stood as toddlers unable to come up with a thought, nor able to articulate the words associated with it. They stood before Nehemiah speechless, convicted for their indiscretions and bad behavior. Nehemiah continued his role prosecuting the case against them.

This part of Nehemiah's story reinforces why it is so important to be people of integrity. It is why Jesus said, we should mean what we say and say what we mean: we should say "Yes, yes" or "No, no" (Matt. 5:37, NASB). James, the brother of Jesus, reiterates His point: "[B]ut your yes is to be yes, and your no, no, so that you may not fall under judgment" (Jas. 5:12b, NASB). To honor God, we must all be people of integrity, who are ready to let our beliefs be evident by the words we say, in the way we act, and to which standard we live.

"Have you no shame?!" he asked. *Are you serious?! Do you not care what your God thinks about you and the way you are behaving. Add to that shame how our godless neighbors are looking at you. They see you to be worse than they are and even more disconnected from the people you once were.* They were not using their God-given authority to serve God; they were serving themselves. Nehemiah was about to teach them the difference.

Levitical law on borrowing money was very specific. Not only were the nobles and officials enslaving their brethren, they were cheating them to get them in bondage. God taught Moses the law, and he delivered it to the people. God wanted His chosen people to deal fairly with each other. If someone needed to borrow money, the guidance was NO excessive usury—for us today, that is like a credit card rate of interest. God did not want the people getting wealthy off of each other in a time of need.

Like the last gas station you pass heading out of town ahead of a hurricane, price gouging is bad. Really bad. God did not want any part of it. Not only were these officials oppressing their fellow countrymen, they were making lots of money off of their misery and misfortune. The people were not borrowing money to invest in a get-rich scheme, they were borrowing to survive…to put food on the table. Nehemiah did not have time for this type of rejection of God's law, and he got his point across.

God's message to Nehemiah was certainly one of patience. God never told Nehemiah this was going to be easy. God did not even tell Nehemiah he was going to survive this effort. Maybe, he was going to start a job he would never finish. He could be killed at any time by enemies, his countrymen, or wild animals. In fact, we do not have a record of any message God gave Nehemiah about *how* to build the wall, what to expect, or if he would be able to complete the job. All we know is God broke Nehemiah's heart, and we are reading the rest of that story and all that building the wall would take…even having to correct his fellow leadership.

When God speaks to us, we need to listen. When I was training for the Marine Corps Marathon in 2019, I had some issues during the lead-up. I went on a 10-day mission trip to Kiev, Ukraine to teach Fellowship of Christian Athletes (FCA) leaders and coaches who are part of the FCA Eurasia program. According to FCA International, they are the gold standard for the world to emulate. Their goal is to proclaim the Gospel of Jesus Christ to transform their nations through coaches and athletes. They do it really, really well.

On our day off from teaching, I had the opportunity to run the Kiev Marathon. I needed a training run while I was on the trip to prepare for the Marine Corps Marathon, and Lindsey was not going to let me go running solo through Ukraine. Our team leader loved the idea of me running the race, and it only cost $60, so I signed up. It was a fun race, but Kiev is the city of seven hills, and there was a significant amount of descending and ascending. My legs got tired out, and I had another marathon in three weeks.

My body was a little beat up after Kiev, and I had to reevaluate my plan to run hard and fast in Washington, D.C. Now, Marine Corps was going to be a run to just have fun and enjoy some sightseeing. There was one problem: rain…lots and lots of rain.

On the day of the race, my legs hurt. The peroneals on each of my legs (muscle attachment area below the knees, on the outside of the legs) was hurting…with every step I took. Additionally, the forecast for the marathon was rain for the entirety of the time I was to be running. Not the best scenario for a marathon, and I had never run two marathons so close together. I was in trouble.

I did what I knew to do…what I was led to do by the Holy Spirit…I prayed. I asked God to heal my legs and get me to the finish line. I also asked for the rain to go away. I didn't want to hurt, and I didn't want to spend the day running through driving rain and puddles. God answered my prayer, sort of. God told me the rain was going to be there for the race, but He also told me my legs would be fine for the race and I would finish with no problems.

God was true to His words. I ran the entire race with no physical limitations. It rained on me from the moment I left the hotel to the last mile of the marathon. It was a driving downpour, so heavy I had limited visibility several times in the race. At the end of my race, the sun came out, and my family and I had a lovely afternoon of sight-seeing. I heard from God, and I was committed to the plan. I ran with confidence…with belief…with faith. Action comes from belief.

Buy-in. Buying in. Being all in. Those words…that sentiment… is a very popular idea. We want people to be invested. When we have a great idea that needs blood, sweat, and tears or we are working hard on a project and need others, buy-in is vital. We need others: we are wired by God to live in community. Other people make us stronger, and we make others stronger. Leadership is about leading *and* being led.

Over every decade of my life, I have worked in leadership development. Being led in a home, on sports teams or a swim team, at my first job, in JROTC, at the Naval Academy, during active duty service, in graduate school, serving churches, participating in regional leadership programs, and living in a family of my own, I continue to be led and to lead.

One program I was involved with recently in southern Georgia was Leadership Lowndes. They exist to educate, train, and develop community leaders. I was a class member and graduated. I was asked to be on the Board of Trustees the next year. I was glad to serve and joined the board.

Over the opening retreat weekend, you meet your 29 classmates and get to know each other…and yourself…through exercises, personality tests, and role-playing. One exercise is a budget challenge. Six teams are formed by the trustees; each team represents the services offered in a community. A common list is education, economic development, defense, local government, quality of life, and health and human services. This role-playing gets fun when participants fully engage their roles, as they fight for their budgetary needs. The wheeling and dealing between groups to accomplish their individual missions is priceless.

I love that exercise because it raises awareness of the connectedness of a community. We depend on each other to survive and thrive. That exercise is instrumental in laying the groundwork for the next ten months of community program days, where the participants learn about all the community has to offer through those six sections of society and others. The class members begin to be committed to each other and start to understand what is needed in their community and how they can make a difference. There is *buy-in*.

Buy-in was necessary for Nehemiah, and it is necessary for the success of Jesus' presence on earth—the Church. Jesus came to save us and transform us—making us more like Him. This we know, but have you ever looked at the purpose of His plan? Sure, you say; John 3:16: "For God so loved the world, that He gave His only begotten son. That whosoever believes in Him will not perish but have eternal life." …everyone knows that. Guys with rainbow wigs and signs at every significant sporting event over the last 40 years know that.

I have always been impressed by the people who championed the *John 3:16* movement. It began in my childhood: signs started popping up at football games in the end zone between the goalposts. Rollen Stewart was his name, and Jesus was his game. Stewart wore a rainbow wig and held a poster-board sign that said simply: John 3:16. That was it. He would sit behind the backboard at NBA games and behind home plate at baseball games. He wanted to be in the camera shot when it was still, locked in on a target. His plan was to get the message out that God loves you and He sent His Son to save you. It is a worthy pursuit, and I cannot begin to imagine how many people looked that verse up or asked what he was doing.

Rollen Stewart wanted the world to know *why* Jesus came: to save the world. …but…how did Jesus do that? We are told by Paul in Ephesians 4 the mission of Jesus followers is two-fold. First, we are to expand the Kingdom of God by reaching people for Jesus. As I told my church, we are not responsible for making people fall in love with Jesus; we just want to set up the date. Jesus does the saving, and Jesus does the second part as well.

The second part of our mission is to deepen the faith of followers. We are to grow as disciples and help others grow on their faith journey as well. Jesus transforms and changes people, but we have a part to play in that as well. Jesus does not expect us to come up with the ways to deepen our faith, He just expects us to follow Him and listen for His voice.

During my years of ministry, I have discovered one of the most difficult aspects to discipleship—following Jesus—is hearing God's prompting and direction. With so many voices flying around us, it can be difficult to hear God giving us guidance. This happens through the power of the Holy Spirit, but we have to be listening and ready to understand. The more we listen for God, the better we get at receiving a message. This is why the *Exerceo Divina* plan requires a quiet response to reading a Bible passage as you exercise. We have to make space for God to talk to us.

I have seen long-time Jesus followers struggle with hearing God, and then there are people who are new to faith that get it early. The greatest example of servant leadership I have seen is my son, Joseph. God communicates to him when there is an opportunity to help someone. It is uncanny how someone from as early as five years of age was able to not only hear from God, but respond. He has a servant's heart. He thinks about what someone else needs as God directs him, and then he does the equally important part of following through with action. It's often easy to know the right thing to do, but it is a whole different thing to actually do it. He can see a situation, and he knows…and acts upon…someone's need.

That is who Jesus is calling him to be. Jesus is beginning that good work in him. Jesus wants to do a good work in you as well. The funny thing about understanding salvation and the Gospel of Jesus is He is the One who defeated death and won the victory for all time, but He is only as powerful in my life as I am willing to let Him be. That is, He is the Savior of the world, but I have to let Jesus save me. I have to commit to His story AND living for Him alone.

Right now, you know like Joseph…like Nehemiah…what needs to be done in your life. Belief in Jesus makes sense and it sounds good, but Jesus came to save us from sin and sometimes from ourselves. Jesus came to show us the way to life by accepting His direction and becoming more like Him. Whatever you need to do right now, God is telling you what needs to be done. You know there are problems, but knowing is not enough. We must commit to changing and *not* becoming the best version of ourselves, but we are to become like Jesus—connected to God, responding to His direction, and filled with divine power to change the world.

Nehemiah was committed, and we learn more about that in the middle of his rebuke (Neh. 5:10, NASB). Nehemiah and his team have been lending these *poor, unfortunate souls* money. They have been helping them survive, helping pay their debt as well as giving them food to eat—grain for bread. Nehemiah says: *This excessive interest—usury—has to stop! On second thought, what you are doing is so bad, you should not only stop gouging them but go one step further. Give back their land and forgive their debt and your claims on future crops. That's right; give them their fields, vineyards, olive groves, and homes. It is the year of jubilee. We are resetting our calendars regardless of the proper number of years since the last time jubilee was celebrated. Today is the day real estate reverts back to the original owner. In keeping with God's plan to keep ancestral homes in a family, and every 50 years, property is restored. That year is now for you corrupt, rich men.* And that was that. Nehemiah got his point across: I do not care about your further support of this construction project. You are breaking God's law, and you cannot have it both ways.

These rich and powerful men were convicted. Nehemiah had his say, and they heard from God that day. Nehemiah spoke God's words right through their ears and into their hearts. They were caught with their hands in the cookie jar, and action was required. In response, they agreed to do everything Nehemiah said they should do. They might have even let the debtors move in with them, if Nehemiah would have suggested it. Then they had church.

Before we continue the story, you may be wondering, why... Why did Nehemiah reach them so quickly? Why did his words cut these rich, successful businessmen to the soul? The answer comes from years of groundwork and investment. Nehemiah worked for years to establish his reputation, leading by example.

For 12 years Nehemiah served as the governor of Judah, he did not take any money from the people. He did not tax them or force them to provide for him. Every governor before him, and probably after him, made each person pay 40 shekels of silver per day (~one pound of silver) to fund a lavish lifestyle of wining and dining. As if that was not enough, those governors also let their appointed authorities shake the people down, forcing them to empty their pockets to make themselves rich as well. This would be like the governor of your state requiring you to pay for his house and his food and then allowing your city's mayor to make you pay for his home as well. No fun...and expensive!

The tax by itself was not a violation of God's law, but Nehemiah knew in the spirit of God's law, profiting off of the oppression of God's people was wrong. He would not and did not make them pay that silver. Nehemiah's officials were not like the usual rabble, because they were not corrupted by their power either. The shake-downs stopped, and the leaders tried leading justly for a change.

Nehemiah explains, they had work to do. They were there to build the wall. They were not there to increase their power/control or to gain property. They were not there to fill their pockets with ill-gotten gain or to climb the ladder of success stepping on the necks of their brothers and sisters. That all sounds nice and good, but you may be wondering why they needed people to buy their meals. He did not eat Ramen noodles in his pajamas; he was the governor of Judah.

Nehemiah was building the wall. Yes, that is true. But his first responsibility was as governor to King Artaxerses—the most powerful man on the planet. Nehemiah had to run Judah. That meant lots of meetings and entertaining regional leaders, visiting dignitaries, and judging legal cases. His primary role to the most powerful king in the world was keep Babylon connected to the states around them through political and diplomatic means. Nehemiah had to keep up his end of the deal that put him into position to fulfill God's calling on his life. We aren't going to get into a discussion about the viability of bi-vocational ministry, but Nehemiah was able to do it well.

Nehemiah fed 150 Jewish leaders and officials at his table in addition to visiting foreign officials. In his home and with his own money, Nehemiah provided for all of those professional, diplomatic responsibilities. How much? Well, it took one ox, six sheep, and some chickens as a daily provision. Not to mention the wine; gallons of wine were delivered every ten days. Nehemiah covered it all because he did not want to make it harder on God's people. Their life was hard enough, and Nehemiah's heart was breaking for them. In all he did for God's people, he was serving God: "Remember me favorably, my God, for all that I have done for this people" (Neh. 5:19, HCSB). He knew God was watching how he was using his power, and he wanted God to be glorified by His people once more.

It was with that credibility, that Nehemiah got the nobles' attention, but they needed to honor their word. Nehemiah called the priests, and they had a sacred moment. It was time to promise to live a new life, before God. They did not need to go to the temple for a big show, and they did not need to wait to make this pledge to God. Instead, Nehemiah called an impromptu worship service.

The priests led the way in addressing God, and since they had already heard the sermon, it was promise-keeping time. Everyone promised to stop this behavior and *do right* from now on. Nehemiah provided the exclamation point: he turned out his pockets, emptying them completely. He said, this is what God will do to ANYONE who breaks the promise they just made. If you break your promise, you will do that exact thing as you struggle to find a single thing of value in your pockets, purses, or money bags. The message was received, and they did what they swore they would do.

In the next chapter we will learn how to avoid traps and pitfalls on our way back to health.

CHAPTER 8

WATCH YOUR STEP

NEHEMIAH WORKED TO KEEP God's people connected to God and on track for the building plan. He had a schedule to keep, for sure, but he also knew what his priorities were. The people had to serve God and abide by His laws—it was who they were. Forgetting that basic truth is what got them into this situation to begin with, and he was not going to let them get away with it on his watch.

Once he got the Jewish leadership back in line, the work continued as it had. The people were succeeding. The plan was working. Nehemiah was proving that with God's direction and provision, a sommelier could be one heck of a construction foreman. Nehemiah was getting it done. The workers knew it.

Yes, Nehemiah was getting it done, but he knew *how* he was getting it done. Nehemiah was there for God, and he was serving God's plan, which meant he had to be completely committed to God. Above everything else, Nehemiah had to rely on God to do what they were doing. God does not ignore a single act of faith or devotion. It never goes unnoticed. It is always recorded and rewarded…in this life or the life to come.

Have you ever been tired? You probably know that feeling of working hard and being emotionally and physically spent. Spiritual exhaustion on the other hand, can be catastrophic. I HAVE BEEN

THERE! Before you go thinking, how could a pastor want to die, I want you to realize no one is immune from attacks from the Enemy, and we are only human after all. Oh yeah, and remember Elijah.

If you are unfamiliar with Elijah, you need to read his story. If you know his story, you can always learn something from hearing it again. Elijah is on the Mount Rushmore of the Jewish people. There was Abraham, Moses, and Elijah. He is the prophet of all prophets, sent by God to speak truth into God's people. He had to speak his mind...I mean, God's mind...to correct and direct and encourage God's people during a very precarious time in their history.

King Ahab was the king of the Northern Tribes—Israel—and he was married to one of the legendarily infamous and diabolic women in the history of the world. Her name was Queen Jezebel, and she was corrupt as corrupt can be. Don't hold it against my wife, Lindsey, but when I met her, she drove a Jeep Cherokee named Jezebel. And she wonders why, before we started dating, I invited her to a Bible study I was teaching because I was worried about her soul. That Cherokee always had a taillight out, which was annoying to the people behind her...and often it was me.

No one had confusion about what Queen Jezebel was going to do. She was from Sidon, located in modern day Lebanon. That means she was a Canannite, and her people loved and served false gods. Chief of those gods were Baal and Asherah. When she married Ahab, she brought devotion to them with her. The King of Israel worshipped and served gods that were offensive to God, and he led the nation into further corruption. Jezebel was driving him and the entire nation into apostasy and rebellion against God. One man was courageous enough to stand firm on the foundation of God: Elijah. He was not following Queen Jezebel, because he knew she had a taillight burned out and was going to lead everyone away from God to death.

Elijah took on 450 prophets of Baal. They had a galactic battle between God and Baal. The Baal prophets offered a sacrifice and called on Baal to ignite the altar from heaven to provide the fire to burn the sacrifice. Elijah offered a sacrifice as well, following God's directions. Spoiler alert: God answered Elijah's prayer and offering. Double spoiler alert: Elijah killed all the prophets of Baal. When Jezebel heard about that, she demanded Elijah be executed, and the hunt was on.

Coming off one of the greatest victories in the history of the world, Elijah was afraid, and he ran. He didn't just run and hide, he asked God to end his life. "But he himself went a day's journey into the wilderness, and came and sat down under a juniper tree; and he requested for himself that he might die, and said, 'It is enough; now, O LORD, take my life, for I am not better than my fathers" (1 Kings 19:4, NASB). This is what it looks like when someone has been overwhelmed by life…and the Devil.

We may find ourselves in this same situation. We begin to make some strides in our health. We are losing weight, or we are getting stronger, or we are eating healthier, or we are incorporating spiritual disciplines into our lives. Then the enemy comes, and we forget our progress. In that one verse (19:4), we learn what emotional exhaustion looks like. We can walk through that one verse and learn ten things from Elijah about what NOT to do in our own struggles and difficulties.

First, Elijah was afraid: he feared Jezebel more than God. He ran away. He let fear overpower him, and he ran for his life. Second, he left God's plan for his life. Third, he left his friends behind. He went off to be alone, cut off from people who could help him.

Fourth, he made a dumb choice: he charged out into the wilderness without a plan. Most of the stories we hear like that end up with someone missing and presumed dead. Fifth, Elijah was already tired, but he went on a journey that would physically, mentally, and spiritually exhaust him, exposing him to an attack from the Enemy. Sixth, he gave up. He quit. He decided his job had been good while it lasted, but it was time to hang it up and file for unemployment. Seventh, he complained to God about all the good he *thought* he was doing that amounted to nothing worthwhile. (You want to talk about a pity party not connected to reality? This was it.) Eighth, he felt defeated. The outcome of the battle with Queen Jezebel and evil had already been decided, and he was the loser. Ninth, he brought up the prophets from the history of Israel, and he compared his ministry to their ministry. (This is always a mistake for servants of God. We never win when we fall into the comparison trap.) Lastly, Elijah decided death was a better option than life. He declared it would be better to be worm food than to serve God and His people anymore. He was spiritually exhausted.

Can you relate to Elijah? Do you feel isolated? Defeated? Lonely? Lost? You are not alone. We all deal with some or all of these ten stages that Elijah went through, but we also have the same solution available to us that was available to Elijah. You may not believe me or even want to hear it, but you are just as important to God as Elijah was. God loves you exactly the same as He loved Elijah or the most *with-it* person you can think of. God cannot love you more, nor will God love you less than He does at this exact moment. God is waiting to hear from you and your cry for help. God responded to Elijah, and He will respond to you.

Elijah called out to God and an angel came to encourage him and feed him. What did God feed him, you ask? The angel baked him a cake and gave him a jar of water. The world always looks better with a little cake…in moderation, of course. After Elijah was nourished, he talked with God. He was nourished and then encouraged with some tough love. Then, God gave him a mission. Elijah was back and better than ever.

It is so easy for us to lose sight of the big picture and fixate on one moment. Maybe we get caught up with what we got wrong instead of what we got right. Our struggle could just come from being exhausted. Working in the world of church planting presented plenty of those opportunities. I would forget about the banner days of high attendance or big public events—defeating the Baal prophets—and think only of the missed phone calls or low attendance days. I would feel exhausted and lost.

When you are tired, everything is more difficult. If you add in spiritual exhaustion, you have a recipe for the Enemy to attack, and that is exactly where Nehemiah was. But Nehemiah knew he had to rely on God, and he did not neglect that relationship.

As the work progressed, enemies took notice. They never stopped keeping tabs on Nehemiah and the workers. They had their spies, and they continued to work against Nehemiah's effort to rebuild the wall. As the wall neared completion, they got desperate, and something had to be done.

Before we moved to Valdosta to start the church, I prayed. Of course, I prayed. I pray every day, but I prayed for God to prepare the ground for us before we got there. A parachute drop is the least effective way to start a church, but that was the model we were sent to emulate. I knew we needed help, and God had to make it happen or nothing would happen. I prayed for God to send us people. I prayed for God to send us people willing to work and committed to His purposes. I needed warm bodies, and I asked God to move inside their chests and for their strength to respond.

About a month after we arrived and started gathering a launch team, I was working in my *cloffice* (walk-in closet/office), and my phone rang. It was a complete stranger who said he heard I was planting a church. I said I was, and he wanted to hear more about it. I asked if we could get together for lunch to talk about it. He agreed. Low and behold he was a sound engineer who had worked with a big church ministry in Atlanta, designing and overseeing their sound operation. He went on to design our whole system and prescribe exactly what power supply and equipment we needed to conduct worship in a functioning movie theater. All that began with, *Let's do lunch.* More people came to us like that—led by God and not even sure what they were getting into, but they came.

Nehemiah prayed a lot. You may be wondering how we know. Well, we see the evidence. God guided Nehemiah's call to leave the only home he had known in Babylon, and God directed and protected Nehemiah as they rebuilt the wall. Perhaps the most important way we see Nehemiah's prayer life produce results was the guidance God gave him about threats.

Let's do lunch. So often, those words can be a good thing. It can be an outing with latent possibilities. There is communion around the table, experiencing God and each other. There can be business deals that bring profits or long-term partnerships. There can be breakup dates as well. Of course, lunch dates can be traps.

Sanballat, Tobiah, and Geshem the Arab (not to be confused with Geshem the Egyptian or Geshem the Philistine or Geshem the Miscreant) kept vigilant in attempting to slow the work on the wall. Even with all of their efforts, the work neared completion. In fact, they finished the wall. The wall was rebuilt! …well…the gates were not hung yet, but the gaps in the wall were gone. *The Three Stooges* had to act, and quickly.

They had a plan: Invite Nehemiah off the wall to join them at their palatial spread for a feast, make one last effort to bribe him and stop the project, and if he rejects them, then kill him. They wanted to meet in Kephirim, in the Ono valley, which would have been around 35 miles away from Jerusalem. They were not dumb, they knew it was a long journey—maybe 10 hours of walking—which would have delayed the work and opened up some other possibilities, if they chose. *It's a dangerous world out there, anything can happen. Wink. Wink.* God was not fooled.

This is why prayer time with God and reliance on His plans is so important. God told Nehemiah something was amiss. God told Nehemiah not to go because it was a trap. Being faithful, Nehemiah did not second-guess God to hear what they had to say. That would have been the practical thing to do...the respectable thing to do...the socially acceptable thing to do. God does not call us to be practical or respectable or acceptable; God calls us to be obedient. Nehemiah knew God wanted him to keep working in Jerusalem, so he rejected their offer, and he did it with a great line.

Nehemiah's choice of words here was epic, and they explained he shouldn't be trifled with. In fact, people have used this answer ever since. When haters hate...when clowns distract...when people try to delay us...when people want to bring us down to their level, simply respond as Nehemiah did. Nehemiah said, "I am doing a great work, and I cannot come down. Why should the work stop while I leave it and come down to you?" (Neh. 6:3bc, NASB). The Stooges sent four...FOUR...invitations. Nehemiah RSVPed, *Will not be attending; I cannot come down from this great work.* This did not go over well with the Stooges.

By the time they sent the fifth invitation, they were fed up. They finally gave up the ruse of a friendly get-together by including an unsealed letter. Much like a letter to the editor in the newspaper, Sanballat included a letter with the invitation. This was important because anyone could read his letter to Nehemiah. And the letter… well, let us just call it what it was: an indictment. Sanballat trumped up some charges, and now he was telling anyone who would listen about what Nehemiah was up to…and it wasn't good.

Sanballat wrote Nehemiah as a *friend*, concerned about his safety. He had heard some rumors, and he just wanted to help Nehemiah out. *Isn't that nice of him?* The rumor on the street was Nehemiah already decided to make himself king, and he bribed some prophets to proclaim him as God's chosen leader. Nehemiah was ready to lead a rebellion against the Babylonians. Lies…all of them, but Sanballat was looking out for Nehemiah, and he wanted to help. He was warning him about the letters that had already been sent to Babylon. He only wanted to meet to come up with a plan. Yeah…right.

Nehemiah responded as he had before: Thanks, but no thanks. He knew they were all lies, and he tried not to panic. He denounced the indictment, and then he did what he had been doing all along: he prayed. He asked God to give him strength (Neh. 6:9c, NASB), and God answered his prayer.

Nehemiah needed strength because the threat was not over yet. The next attack came from a friend—a trusted ally—who came to *protect* Nehemiah. Shemaiah was the keeper of the East Gate, and he invited Nehemiah to a secret meeting. That would have been fine, but the location he picked was a trap. It was not because of any danger around the meeting, it was about what the location said about Nehemiah.

Shemaiah attempted to gain Nehemiah's confidence by telling him there was a plot to kill him and they needed to hide. He wanted to use God's temple as a holy shield against attack…an attack Shemaiah said was imminent and would be deadly. He picked God's house because it was traditionally a safe house—a sanctuary—against harm. Shemaiah wanted him to move into the temple and hide there. Sure, Nehemiah would probably be safe, but the optics were all wrong.

Think about what it would say about Nehemiah if he had to use God's house as a shield. It would mean he was so intimidated, so scared by his enemies, that he could not face them like a man. The enemies were so strong, and Nehemiah was so weak that he could no longer finish building the wall because he was hiding in the temple. It would have meant he no longer relied on God's provision and protection, and hiding in the temple would have been a statement that saving his own life was more important than God's plan for Israel. He would have been hiding in the corner of a dark room, crying and lamenting his woes.

Nehemiah would lose all credibility, and God's work would go unfinished. He was not a priest. He could not live in the temple and act like it was his home. He had no work to do there; his work was on the wall and in the courts and meeting rooms as Governor of Judah. God revealed it all: the false messages of the prophetess Noadiah, Shemaliah's lies, and the other prophets who were speaking against him. All of them—funded by Sanballat and Tobiah—were bribed to stop God's work and eliminate Nehemiah and his efforts. Nehemiah prayed for strength, and he prayed God would fight against his enemies.

God answered Nehemiah's prayers, because not long after this episode, the wall was completed. This part of the story is what speaks so strongly to me regarding commitment and perseverance. How often do we get 90% of the way to our goal? The last 10% completes the task, so we would be 100% done. But we get tired. We get worn out. We come off message. We slow down, and we can be so close to finishing. It is right there, but we have to realize our goals and dreams.

Ed Orgeron is an American football coach. He is from Louisiana and of Cajun descent, and he loves his home state. His dream was to play football in Death Valley Stadium at Louisiana State University (LSU). He signed with LSU out of high school, but he never played a down in a game for LSU football. He did not reach that goal; he got close, but he didn't reach it. His new dream was to coach football on the biggest stage and in the toughest conference—The Southeastern Conference (SEC). Maybe he could even win a title at LSU.

Orgeron coached all over the country, and at the highest levels at the universities of Miami, Syracuse, Tennessee, and Southern California. He fought against alcoholism and has been sober for 20 years. He was even hired as the coach of the University of Mississippi in 2005. It did not work out. In fact, Coach Orgeron shot himself in the foot more times than he would care to admit with off-the-field struggles. He was fired, and then he bounced around the top level of college football as a coordinator.

Orgeron realized something needed to change if he was going to reach his goals. He changed his approach. He had always been fiery, but he channelled those emotions into concern and care for his players. The stories from coaches who worked with him and his former players are near legend at this point. Either dragging his sons to the practice facility to run defensive line drills on a Saturday when they said they were bored to showing up at in-home recruiting trips asking, "Mama, where's the gumbo?", Coach O has a way of doing things. Right before a big game, the team has its own pep rally. To get the team fired up one time, Orgeron came in with two Red Bull energy drinks. He ripped off his shirt during his speech and shotgunned the Red Bulls. His players love him for it.

Orgeron took over LSU with the interim tag when the head coach was fired midseason. Three years later in 2019, he led LSU to an unbeaten record, coached a Heisman Trophy winning quarterback, and the team won a national title. If he had not taken the job at LSU as the defensive coordinator and thrived when he had the opportunity, who knows what would have happened.[41]

No matter how close we get to our goals, we have to go the whole distance to achieve them. Faced with another threat, God told Nehemiah this was a trap. Nehemiah told Shemaiah absolutely, he was not going to use God's house as a shield, and he would finish what he started out in the open, for all to see. God did not disappoint.

Just 52 days…that's days not weeks…52 days after they started building the wall, they completed the job. It was the twenty-fifth day of Elul. The completed wall was like a medal on God's chest. Nehemiah's enemies would not be confused about what just happened. They were the ones who were filled with fear, and the wind went completely out of their sails. Tobiah and others did not relent until the wall was completed. They had continued to write letters to the Jewish nobles, attempting to subvert the work of Nehemiah. They failed. Nehemiah succeeded, but there was still work to be done as Nehemiah struggled to stay on task, keeping God's people in God's will…and every detail was important.

Nehemiah accomplished what no one thought he could do, nor even fathomed how quickly it could be done. The wall was finished.

The gates—controlling access to the city—were in place for the first time in 250 years. Imagine what that would have felt like. The holy city of God had walls again, protecting God's people and the house of God. While Nehemiah's job as foreman was ending, his role as governor was going to get quite busy, quite quickly.

Nehemiah would have learned a great deal about leadership and politics from serving in the king's court, but God did the perfecting work to make him the leader he grew to be. Nehemiah had to have people he trusted, so he started with family. His brother Hanani—who first reported to him about the conditions of Jerusalem—comes back into the story in a big way. Hanani, along with the captain of the citadel (city defense), Hananiah, were placed in charge of Jerusalem itself—it's defense and daily operations. Nehemiah trusted his brother, and Hananiah was selected because of his devotion to God. As Nehemiah says, "[H]e was an honest man and feared God more than most men" (Neh. 7:2b, MSG). Don't ask me about what a coincidence it is that the two guys Nehemiah put in charge of Jerusalem have nearly identical names: Hanani and Hananiah. Both names come from the same origin as my daughter Hannah's name: Grace. Their names tell us *God is gracious*, and by their position, Nehemiah declared the wall and the city were being rebuilt by the grace of God.

God's people were changing just as their country was as well; so was Nehemiah. Nehemiah's transformation can be so easy to miss during this journey. Nehemiah was someone trained in growing and processing grapes. He probably would have been able to leave Babylon and get a job at one of the finest wineries in France or Northern California. He had mad skills understanding grapes and wine. He knew what it took to grow wine that tasted wonderful, and he knew what bad wine tasted like as well. Nehemiah's palate was well-developed, and he knew what the king and his court liked and didn't like. Nehemiah could have lived out the rest of his life living a comfortable life in palaces, serving whoever was the sovereign. He could have.

Once Nehemiah heard from God and responded, the transformation began. God gifted him for the tasks that lay before him, and God prepared the way by giving him the earthly authority, through the king, to take on his new responsibilities. Nehemiah went from a vinedresser to a master architect, accomplished builder, leader of men and women, and the governor of a growing nation. Whatever life Nehemiah lived before God called him fell away, and Nehemiah grew in faith and standing, becoming who God knew him to be.

My experience of God's faithfulness is similar to what I see in Nehemiah. God has led me back from my brokenness to healing and restoration. You may be at the beginning of such a process or right in the midst of it. Just as Nehemiah is being rebuilt, so are all of us as Jesus followers. Jesus has called us, and when we respond, we are equipped and sent to do great things. Bit by bit, brick by brick, day by day, detail by detail, and decision by decision, God is working on our behalf and leading us to wholeness. Just like Nehemiah, we will have what we need to do what God asks us to do. God has entrusted us with a gifting, and we have work to do.

With Nehemiah's trusted men guarding Jerusalem, he gave them their orders. No one was to come in or out of the city at night. They had worked too hard and too many hours to act as if they did not have walls or gates. The gates would be guarded around the clock, and the watchmen were to be selected from those living by the individual gates. Again, Nehemiah wants people devoted to God, but he also knew people would be a bit more determined in their security duties when they know their families and their homes are near the gate for which they are responsible. The city was finally secure.

Nehemiah began restoring life back to what should be *normal*. Priests and others needed for temple operations were empowered and assigned. The city was secure, but it resembled ruins more than actual buildings. There were not many people able to live there, and those living in Jerusalem were very spread out. Nehemiah wanted an accounting for the population, so he went to the record of who *should* be living there.

The first group of exiles from Babylon returned not long after 538 BCE (Before the Common Era—what many know as BC (Before Christ)) when Cyrus the Great of the Persian Empire sent out his Great Edict. He declared conquered people were allowed to go home. Nehemiah consulted the genealogy of those who returned to Jerusalem and Judah, repopulating their hometowns. They were led by Zerubbabel and others. Nehemiah used the record to establish a baseline census of the people identified by either their family of origin or place of origin, priestly families, or those who were sent for temple service. Jerusalem needed to function as the capital city for God's people, and that meant *people* were needed to bring activity and life to those hallowed streets once again.Nehemiah studied the record to determine those who returned in the first wave who did not have the necessary documentation to support their citizenship. Nehemiah was a leader who got things done, but he was not interested in cutting corners or doing the wrong thing. In their defense, there was destruction and uncertainty after the Babylonian siege, so missing documentation was a legitimate issue. The priests consulted the holy dice and how they would cast lots to make God-dependent decisions—Urim and Thummim—to determine if some of the people with questionable family records were legitimate members of the Jewish family or not.

With all of that accounting work done, the final total number of the returning exiles was 42,360, who would become known as The People of Israel. Additional slaves and animals—horses, mules, camels, and donkeys—made the trip as well. The governor, the heads of families, and anyone who could, made monetary offerings and donated the items needed for worship to begin once the Temple altar was built. With the lost ten tribes of the Northern Kingdom gone forever, this group of exiles and those that were left by the Babylonians (in 586 BCE), were the people God wanted to use to put Israel back on the map, literally.

In the next chapter, we will see how important it is to focus on every part of God's plan.

CHAPTER 9

"FOCUS, DANIEL-SAN. FOCUS."

WATCHING *THE KARATE KID* was a formative experience for me and my generation as we realized the strongest and biggest don't always win. Daniel Laruso, from New Jersey, was able to defeat the golden boy…literally…he had golden locks, money, and a cool motorcycle. You might even have wanted to be Johnny if he wasn't such a jerk. Daniel won the karate tournament and the girl, all while being led by a great instructor and life coach. He even won a sequel; while not as good as the first movie, there are still some good lessons…and new karate cinematic technique in *The Karate Kid Part II.*

Mr. Miyagi and Daniel head to Okinawa to check on Mr. Miyagi's ailing father. While there, an old foe comes looking for Miyagi, and Daniel has a new enemy to defeat. In a stand-off between the two sides, Daniel has been forced into a competition in a bar with a heavy wager on the outcome. Daniel has to *karate chop* through six horizontally stacked one inch plates of ice. At the climax of the scene, Daniel pulls Mr. Miyagi to the side and gets mad at him for putting him in this difficult situation. Daniel is annoyed, having seen other men bigger than him fail at breaking their plates of ice, and he asks, "What do you expect me to do?!" In a variation of Mr. Miyagi's famous message from *The Karate*

Kid: "Focus." Daniel asks, "Oh, great! What are you going to do?!" Miyagi says, "Pray." Daniel prays, breathes, and focuses before he attempts the impossible challenge. Success! He chops through all six plates of ice and wins the money, sticking it to Miyagi's old foe.[42]

Focus was needed for Daniel's challenge, but Mr. Miyagi's response of "Pray" is priceless. Ha! Good stuff. God can do amazing things with prayer and focus. If I had a dollar for every time I have told my nine-year-old son to focus, I would be a rich man. He is not the only one that has trouble focusing. If I had a dollar for every time God has told ME to focus, I would have more money than I can count. It is easy to lose focus, and it was no different for God's people.

Life settled down in Israel. The temple was functioning, and the wall was secure and doing its job. God's chosen people were centering life in Jerusalem once again. There was, however, one thing missing. The overwhelming majority of people did not know their own history, and they did not know what their covenant with God was about. They did not know what God expected of them, or how the law was established and what it required. With their construction project completed, Nehemiah knew the people needed more than a wall to unite them.

More than land, a temple, or a wall, God had a plan to unite His people. From the beginning of Israel as a nation, God promised to honor their covenant if they kept His law. Moses came down with the Law and requirements for God's covenant with them. In Exodus 19:5-6a, God gives Moses a message for the people: "Now then, if you will indeed obey My voice and keep My covenant, then you shall be My own possession among all the peoples, for all the earth is Mine; and you shall be to Me a kingdom of priests and a holy nation." From the beginning of their relationship with God, the nation of Israel was defined by keeping up their end of God's covenant. God is always faithful, but their downfall began when they did not keep up their end.

As life in Israel settled back to some version of normalcy in post-exile Jerusalem, Nehemiah began to realize for the wall to effectively protect them from physical threats, there had to be some spiritual rebuilding as well. The wall was completed near the end of the month Elul, and the re-opening of the city gates brought life back to Jerusalem and the Jewish people. Now, it was time for the people to realize who they were. Nehemiah went to Ezra the priest, and they came up with a plan.

Ezra knew the Law. He was a priest, and he lived and breathed the Law. There was a festival on the calendar that went back to the days of Moses, who was considered the greatest leader/prophet by the Jewish people. They had not celebrated the Feast of Booths since they were forced out of the Promised Land by the Babylonian hoards; mainly because it involved a pilgrimage to Jerusalem. The purpose of the feast was to remind the nation of Israel that they had not always had a homeland and they traveled in the wilderness. In those days, they lived in tents, and God's house was a tabernacle—a tent with wood framing with fabric draped over the frame—which the Levites set up and took down every time God said to move.

The Feast of Booths is still an opportunity today for Jewish people to build temporary booths with wood frames of thick branches and cover them with palm fronds and willow branches. They can still see through the makeshift roofs to the stars, and some Jews even sleep under them at night. The festival lasts for seven days with a separate celebration following on the eighth day called the Great Hosanna. From the partial conquest of the

Promised Land through Jesus' day, Rabbi Zimmerman shares male Jews would travel the pilgrimage to Jerusalem for three festivals: Passover, Pentecost, and the Feast of Booths.[43]

At this momentous time in the life of the people of Israel, Ezra and Nehemiah thought it was the perfect festival at that time. Adding to the timing of the new wall and the new temple, Solomon's Temple was dedicated at the Feast of Booths. What was always an occasion for Jewish people to reconnect with God and their faith would be such a day once again.

Nehemiah threw a party, and he invited every resident of Israel to join him. He had a big wooden platform built, and he started planning for their arrival. And they came…in droves…every man and woman in Israel…anyone capable of understanding. Ezra brought out the Book of the Revelation of Moses (Neh. 8:2), or what we know as a version of the book Exodus.

The people were starting to understand the gravity of this moment. When Ezra opened the scrolls, the people began to worship. They stood where they were, and a worship service broke out. While standing or kneeling, people had their hands raised to God, and they sang any hymn they knew. Whether it was a traditional song that was a distant memory or if they were moved by God to impromptu singing, the people praised and worshipped God.

Ezra read from dawn until noon. He was flanked on either side by Levites, all men of learning who knew the Law as well. The people hung on every word as if God was speaking directly to them. In fact, God was doing just that. The Levites dispersed throughout the crowd to begin to interpret what Ezra was reading. Much like a preacher whose purpose is to hear God's message in a passage of Scripture and relate it to the congregation he serves, the priests were connecting God's people with His message. Some of the congregation needed help with the *Hebrew*, while others were missing a word here or there, but the Levites translated and explained the message. The people heard God's Word and they began to understand exactly what they—as a people—had done to the God who loved them...to the God Who was reviving their nation.

Nehemiah was right there in the midst of the small group of leaders with Ezra and the Levites. He was leading God's people back home in more ways than one. He felt the emotion from the crowd. He saw the recognition on their faces. He witnessed the clarity of thought as their heads nodded in agreement. He also noted that they began moving in a negative direction.

The people began to be convicted. They became critical of themselves, seeing only the negativity and discrepancies between who God called them to be and who they actually were. This is something I am very good at myself; sometime I think I am perfect at finding my imperfections. As an Enneagram Type One, I am a perfectionist.

While the Enneagram has been around for hundreds, if not thousands of years, many people are not aware of what this personality classification system is, and even more incorrectly think they know what the Enneagram is about. The system consists of nine personality types that classify people, who have been formed by their environment and who they needed to be to function in that environment. Each type has a healthy state and an unhealthy state. The goal is for people to learn about themselves to avoid the slide into disintegration—unhealth—and work toward the healthier, integrated self.

While Ones are called perfectionists, I like *Reformer*, but that language is not as commonly utilized when describing Type Ones.

The Enneagram is a means to describe personality types to better understand each other but also ourselves. Ones immediately see every flaw. When I say we see every flaw, I do not simply mean we notice when someone makes an odd choice when loading the dishwasher or has a piece of thread on their clothes. I mean we know when things are not *right*, like you cannot help but notice you are wet when you fall into a pool.

For a more current example, during the COVID19 pandemic changes to grocery shopping procedures, many stores went to one-way traffic through the store—down one aisle and up the next. When a One is following the directions—pushing their cart in the correct direction—and we see someone blatantly violating the rules and pushing their cart in the opposite direction, we are having a fit on the inside (we are annoyingly aware our clothes are wet from the pool with no way to dry off). Our first inclination is to move toward the middle of the aisle to prevent the destructive criminal from passing us by. And that is the good inclination; the negative (although we don't think it is *that* negative) inclination is to slam their cart into the stacks of canned goods. Did I mention we have an anger issue? In our defense, after that episode, we would put all of the cans back in order because it was the right thing to do, ensuring the cans were all placed back in their proper spots, uniformly on the shelves.

Some of us fixate on each infraction, and others are able to balance awareness of flaws with tolerance of them. Healthy Ones can be great reformers and activists—leading people toward change and the ideal. Unhealthy Ones can lash out at everyone because of their own failings and being hyper-critical of the faults they see in others.

Not that they were all Ones, but the people of Israel felt their failings as Ezra read the Law to them. The people of Israel became very aware of their faults, and they were not able to get away from them. They knew in an overwhelming way that they and their ancestors had rejected God, and they got what they deserved. They were very much in the wrong, and they had no ability to make it right. Here was a great teaching moment for Nehemiah and the other leaders.

It was a lesson in forgiveness. This is where many of us are right now: in need of forgiveness. We need to ask God to forgive us for letting things get so bad, for not honoring our bodies, minds, and souls as the gifts from God they are. We also need to forgive ourselves for making bad choices and ignoring the mistakes as they piled up, creating a barrier between us and God. Israel needed to do this as well.

Nehemiah, Ezra, and the Levites began to explain to the people the nature of God and the blessings of second chances. God had given the Promised Land back to them, and now they needed to appreciate it. For the first time in a long time, Israel was the nation God wanted them to be. Nehemiah said, "This day is holy to God, your God. Don't weep and carry on" (Neh. 8:9, MSG). He sent them home, and he told them to get ready for a party...a big party...a feast. Think of the biggest family reunion you ever attended. For our older hippie friends, think about Woodstock, and for our younger hippie friends, think about Bonnaroo...without the drugs and unbridled sex. Everybody that they knew was about to come together for a blowout, and the purpose was to praise God. It was like a church service started, and it turned into Super Bowl week.

Nehemiah told them to go home and start cooking and preparing for the party. The Levites helped teach the people about moving from sorrow to joy. They were not to be oblivious to their sinfulness, but they needed to realize that God loved them even with their checkered past. Without the recognition of God's love and willingness to forgive—both from hearing Ezra read The Book of the Revelation of Moses and the Levites' explanation to Nehemiah's call to rejoice—the people would not have established the new foundation they would need to once again be God's people.

They celebrated. They gathered their family and ate and drank to the glory of God. They told stories and counted their blessings. Those who had enough, invited those who did not. Neighborhood block parties popped up all over Israel, and they praised God through it all.

The next day, Nehemiah gathered Ezra, the priests, the Levites, and the elders of Israel for a meeting. It was time to start building again, but this time it was about a connection that brought the leaders of Israel to God. This was a Bible study. It was a small group meeting. It was a covenant group. The leaders gathered together to look at The Revelation, and they realized today was the day to rediscover a tradition.

They learned about the Feast of Booths and what was required. Nehemiah and Ezra prepared a decree, and the elders made sure it got disseminated. They sent it throughout Jerusalem and to every town. The decree told them to gather up any type branch they could to build a booth; each family got to work. They built booths on the roofs of their homes and in courtyards. They built booths in the courtyard of the Temple of God, at the Water Gate plaza, and the Ephraim Gate plaza—important, public spaces where people congregate. Every single person in Israel had access to a booth. They could put their eyes on them, touch them, and feel what the night air was like under them as they looked at the stars through the branches.

This particular celebration of the Feast of Booths was groundbreaking for the people of Israel as they rediscovered what it was to be a nation with a place to worship God—the Temple—and walls around their capital city. They were not only ushering in a new era filled with pride in their identity as God's children, but the people also were able to connect with their ancestors, remembering the victories and miracles that helped shape them. God did it all by communicating with them through their minds, bodies, and souls. They constructed the booths, feeling the wood and the palm fronds; their minds raced with ideas and memories as they looked into the heavens through the branches that provided their shelter; and their spirits were moved through the connection to their ancestors as they felt their spirits lying next to them under the stars. God certainly loves to use all parts of us to communicate His message and love.

The people left their homes for a week, and slept under the booths. They reflected on who their ancestors were, and more importantly, who they were at that moment. They appreciated the Temple of God, where they could worship freely, a freshly built wall around Jerusalem, and the new beginnings of a nation with great potential. The Feast of Booths had not been celebrated since the people ignored the practice after Joshua led them into the Promised Land, but the practice was restored that day.

Restoring your life to what God intends for you will not be easy. Doing what needs to be done will take time and repetition. Malcolm Gladwell, a very engaging and thought-provoking author, explains what it takes to be successful. He studied what it took to succeed across many different disciplines in his book *Outliers*.

Gladwell studied hockey and soccer players, computer science pioneers, geniuses, and mathematicians to mention just a few. He found something that contributed to being a success at something that we can all take and adapt to our own circumstance.

Gladwell relays the *10,000-hour Rule*. It takes 10,000 hours of work at a task to become an expert. Across disciplines in academics, athletics, music, and other fields, Gladwell sees a factor that connects all those participants with success: practice….10,000 hours to be exact, which the research suggests takes at least ten years. Gladwell shares a flawed view of success: "Achievement is talent plus preparation."[44] He argues talent is not as important as preparation. Pianists and violinists were studied. Those musicians with varying levels of success all began playing at roughly the same age: five years old. What distinguished their growth towards success was not their instructor or where they studied; it was how many hours they practiced. Researchers found the elite performers separated from others by the age of twenty, when they reached the 10,000-hour standard. "Ten thousand hours is the magic number of success."[45] Reaching that number takes many years, but we are not talking about becoming expert cellists but healthier people.

Preparation is what we need to focus on for lasting change. We are not talking about getting on a diet to lose a certain number of pounds. That idea implies a short-term goal with a very clear start day and finish day. Being holistically healthy the way God intended is a lifestyle; it is a way to live every day. We want to develop a system that is repeatable that involves engaging God through exercise, what and when we eat, and our commitment to God's intentions for us. We are not trying to accrue 10,000 hours of effort, but we are attempting to incorporate God into every part of our life. Ten-thousand hours seems like a large amount of time because it is a large amount of time. The lesson of the 10,000-hour Rule is not telling us to not try if we cannot get to that number. No, the lesson of that rule is if we invest ourselves and our time into a repeatable process we will see results. It will become second nature, and the health change we are making, as hard as it may seem at times, will become doable and impactful. Repetition is how we foster significant change and discover who God desires us to be.

God's people need repetition and preparation. Every day of the seven days, Ezra read from the scroll of The Revelation. They learned about God each day. They heard what God's Word sounded like, and the Levites explained what it meant to them and how they were to live honoring God. They ate and drank in community. They slept in the booths; every day of the seven days. On the eighth day, they came back together as the Law required in Leviticus 23, and they offered sacrifices to God. The nation was being rebuilt.

Nehemiah knew in the heart of the Law, there is a promise. As the lion Aslan tells Susan and Lucy in *The Lion, the Witch, and the Wardrobe* there is a "Deeper Magic" that governs. When Aslan is sacrificed in the place of the traitor Edmund, the White Witch assumes she has won the final victory over her only rival, Aslan. She knew the Deep Magic—the law—but she did not know the words that wrote that law; Aslan did…and so did Nehemiah.

Moses prepared to end his tenure as the leader of God's chosen people by explaining what fulfillment of God's Law looked like and why it was necessary to maintain their connection with God. In Deuteronomy 31:10-13, Moses tells the people how important it is to celebrate the Feast of Booths. It was meant to be a time when the people—men, women, children, and the aliens among them—heard the story of God's relationship with Israel. The story was to be told to all gathered there, "[S]o that they may hear and learn and fear the LORD your God" (Deut. 31:12b, NASB). It is a great opportunity to teach those who have not heard God's story how powerful it is and the life it provides.

Most of the people did not know the story. Now that the people had a semblance of a nation with borders and walls, it was time to build a wall around each of their hearts. These walls would not be to prevent them from loving others or being loved. That is what we think about today when we hear about a wall around a heart: resistance to romantic love because of a prior wound, or those that wall others out because of fear of the unknown. No, these walls were necessary, and not to defend them from the harm others can cause. These walls would be about the damage they could do with their actions in rebellion.

Guardrails are important on our journey. Pastor Andy Stanley preached a popular sermon series by the same name. He used the idea of guardrails on the side of the road at dangerous curves or near steep drop-offs. Those guardrails are necessary because without them, we could drift into a situation that is difficult to rectify or repair. We can drive right off the road, and once we leave the path we were on, we may never be able to get back nor recover from the fall.

If we struggle with sexual sin, having unlimited access to the Internet can be dangerous. We need someone to have complete access to our computers, checking caches and search histories. If we deal with substance abuse issues, we cannot be left alone to figure it out. We need someone who will check on us and ask the hard questions. If we become consumers in our relationship with God, we have to know others who can speak grace and truth into our lives to help us stay committed to God's purposes.

"People…they're the worst." This is one of my favorite lines from comedian Jerry Seinfeld. I do not know Jerry Seinfeld, but I feel like I do. I have seen every episode of the television series "Seinfeld" many times as I have his Netflix series "Comedians in Cars Getting Coffee." (I actually started watching them before Netflix picked them up when they were available exclusively at the website of the same name. I'm a big fan.) I have seen his comedy act in person on two different occasions. This quote from his television show is one of my favorites.

He is a One on the Enneagram, like me, so I get his humor on a deeper level. Ones are always immediately aware of the problems in any room they walk into. We know the papers that are stacked a little off, the shoes left on the floor (with the laces not tucked into the shoes), the table setting that is not symmetrical nor matches all of the other settings around it, anything adrift in the room, the speck of dust on the floor, … I could go on. And do not get me started if there are people in the room, the list will blossom once people show up and start talking, saying things that are incorrect or annoying. The good days are when we keep our mouths shut about the infractions, and the bad days are the ones when we cannot stop ourselves from sharing all that is wrong in a space or the people in that space.

"People, they're the worst." Yep. That says it all. We have problems. Bunches. Mountains. If you don't think you do, let me hang out with you for a few minutes. Really. It will be therapeutic…I promise.

Why do we struggle so much? I'm glad you asked. In my many years of *research* as a One and a pastor, I have found two truths about human nature. First, we focus on ourselves too much, and second, we lie to ourselves a lot. Most of our failings can be linked to one of those two things. We are either listening to our own desires over God's voice, or we fool ourselves into thinking this little *cheat* here and there will not hurt me—one more Twinkie, one last shot, a few more minutes on that website or app. All of it is rebellion from God, and God will not allow rebellion without consequences.

God tells us what He is about through the story of the Jewish people in the First Covenant—the Old Testament—and the New Covenant—the New Testament. God claimed the people of Israel when they were slaves in Egypt and saved them. Then God gave them the rules He wanted them to follow. They did not do so well. They could never seem to get their heads around the First Commandment: "No other gods, only Me." It really is the one that gives purpose and meaning to the other commandments. They could not do it, and their kingdoms were destroyed because of it.

Jesus came to redeem not only Israel, but to open up all the world to the promises of God. Instead of speaking through other people, God came down in flesh to teach us about His love and show us how to live. But it always goes back to Rule #1: No other gods, but Me. As Jesus told the rich young ruler in Mark 10, get rid of your distractions, which you have lots of, and come follow Me. Our undivided attention is all God has ever wanted, and it is what He still wants.

Undivided begins with me first. Sure, we have money, cars, toys, trips, activities, and other *no gods* like us to distract us, but we have a bigger problem: ourselves. At the head of the line of *no gods* fighting for my attention and my way is…me. I like what I like. I like to do what I want to do, and I focus on those things almost exclusively. I like to go where and when I want to go. God does not like that, nor does God work like that.

A Hall of Fame American football player sums this up better than I ever could. Terrell Owens (T.O.) was a wide receiver for multiple teams. He was the best in the league at his position more than once and was a five-time first-team All-Pro selection. Owens ranks third all-time in NFL receiving yards and touchdowns. Wide receivers are known to be self-centered. They line up in formations away from the rest of the team. They score on their own, not normally relying on blockers to move people out of their way. Terrell Owens was a great receiver, but he was not the humblest of people.

Owens explained his motivation…and a broader theological statement without knowing it. T.O. was infatuated with himself, and he never really felt appreciated by his teammates, fans, or the media. Known for over-the-top touchdown celebrations, he carried those to the bench. More than once, Owens said, "I love me some me!" *I love me some me.* Yeah. That is about right. We all live our lives like, *We love us some us.* Well, God loves us. God loves us enough to let us live our lives that way, but that is a violation of His commandments and a rejection of the life Jesus offers. Living with ourselves at the center of our lives does not work for long.

With awareness of our ego-centric leanings—the desire to focus on ourselves first—we need to redirect our attention. To reverse the struggles we all deal with, we have to change the way we do things. To say it in a more positive way: to address our difficulties in life, (1.) we need to focus more on the needs of others, and (2.) we need to be honest with ourselves. Life change happens through those two commitments.

The people of Israel had to build some walls around their hearts as guardrails to keep the other gods out. They needed to wall off those non-gods they worshipped for so long and for whom they betrayed God. A common theme throughout the destruction of

Israel and Judah was of a husband with a wayward wife. She would *play the harlot* and give herself to everyone but her husband. The prophet Hosea actually lived out Israel's choices.

If you have never read the book Hosea, you need to do it. First, you will be amazed that God asked someone to do what God asked Hosea to do. Second, you will be shocked that someone *did* what God asked Hosea to do. Third, you will be exceedingly thankful God has not asked you to do what He asked Hosea to do.

Hosea had to live out the rebellion of the Jewish people. God told Hosea to take a wife of harlotry. Of course, we don't use that word too much anymore, but she was a woman of the night, involved in…so to say…the oldest profession. He was to marry a woman named Gomer, and she was a prostitute. Next, they were to have children together. Then she would reject Hosea and the children to go back to her former life as a prostitute. Then, Hosea took her back. This is the story of God's relationship with the nation of Israel. Hosea lived out what God had suffered through for generations with His people. Gomer is who they are, and that is why they needed a wall.

It was time to repent. Nehemiah tells us it was the 24th day of the same month when they participated in a day similar to Yom Kippur, or the Day of Atonement, which is celebrated by Jews around the world, observed annually on a designated day between mid-September and early October. Atonement can be thought of as *at-one-ment* because it brings us back into union—at-one—with God. Atonement is good to help with our two-part change process, because it requires focus and honesty.

The people were repenting of their former life apart from God and the sins they celebrated instead of mourned. The people fasted. They put on burlap and got so down into the dirt, they smudged their faces with it. This was not a figurative reference to submission; the people got into the dirt to confess and repent of their sins. They confessed their own sins and those of their ancestors. They stood and knelt and laid flat on their faces. They cycled through those positions, rising to praise God and lowering themselves to show their confessions meant something, remembering what they and their people had done to God.

Standing, kneeling, and lying prostrate...these were the postures they took with their bodies. Being on your knees with your face on the ground to God is normally the easy part. Do not get me wrong, it can be a hard thing for people to learn to bow their knees to God or anyone else, for that matter. Bowing to God physically is important, but it will never be as important as assuming that position spiritually and mentally. Going through the motions is something we all know a little about—we have either done it or seen it. Physically lowering yourself to the ground by bending your knees is anatomically possible for most people, but that gesture means nothing without the mind and soul submitting to God. Sure, it looks like you are showing your allegiance to God, but looks can be deceiving.

God wants all that we are, but the physical signs are easy to mask. We can pretend to take the correct posture, but hearts and minds that are wholly devoted to God cannot be faked. The prophet Joel said, "And rend your heart and not your garments" (Joel 2:13a, NASB). Kneeling is as visible as tearing your shirt and also as easy. Unless you have one of the retro denim shirts (or you kept your original one from the 1980s), those shirts are not as easy to tear; I digress. Nehemiah and Ezra knew as a nation they had to rend their hearts, beg for forgiveness, and start again. The Levites called the people to their feet, and the hymn of contrition began—their song of repentance and life-change.

Nehemiah prayed the hymn with emotion and conviction. He started at the beginning of God's story to recount all that God had done and what Israel had done in response to God's love and mercy. He began with creation, praising God for the heavens, the seas, and the life that filled the earth. He moved to Abraham's call and migration to Canaan and the promised, eventual home of his descendants, and God kept His word. God saw His people in bondage in Egypt, and He delivered them through the leadership of Moses—one of the greatest events in human history and a defining moment for the Israelites. God guided them with a pillar of smoke by day and fire by night as millions trekked through the desert not knowing where they were going or what awaited them when they arrived. When they were ready, God gave them the Law. Even conquering the Egyptians and thriving in the wilderness did not keep Israel from complaining and rebelling with other gods. They forgot God's faithfulness so quickly, and they suffered because of their short memories.

Back and forth they went—following God and rejecting God—never consistently in relationship with God. They arrived in the Promised Land and were rewarded with their own homes as God cleared the Canaanite enemies from their midst. How soon they forgot…Israel lusted for other gods and the women of other nations. When God's messengers—the prophets—came bringing God's correction, they ignored them as long as they could stand it and killed them when they could not tolerate the sound anymore. They were so committed to false gods, God's Word became fingernails on a chalkboard.

When they came to their senses and begged for God's intervention, He would send a savior to get them back on track or to rid their land of an enemy. When life got comfortable and prosperous again, a new form of rebellion came—worse than before. Finally, the Assyrians destroyed the Northern Tribes, forever to be known as the *Ten Lost Tribes* because of their complete destruction and exile to the ends of the earth. The people of Judah did not learn from their kin, and nearly 200 years later, they were conscripted into slavery by the Babylonians. They were in a suzerain/vassal treaty with foreign kings—subservient, paying for protection with crops and tribute.

Israel had once been a nation that contended with nations as equals. Now, superpowers owned the Jewish people and their land. Extortion was their way of life. They were once slaves who were given a *land flowing with milk and honey*, which they turned into a nation, and now they were slaves again who barely had an identity beyond a footnote in the history of other nations.

A handful of Levites explained these events as Nehemiah recounted them. They explained the severity of these infractions, and what this rejection did to God. They detailed how God gave them chance after chance and opportunity after opportunity to come back into relationship with God. All of God's chasing after Israel was to no avail, and that is why they were in burlap and covered with dirt. Their confession and contrition was the beginning, but repentance was required to realize God's promises once again.

As the people began to own their guilt, they got quite upset. They may have even been more distraught than the leaders expected—more honesty than the people were ready for. Nehemiah, Ezra, and the Levites saw the emotion and concern on the faces of the people. It began to look like they were losing a grasp on the aspect of hope that comes with confession and repentance. Yes, people are sinful, and they do bad things, but God is gracious. God forgives. That was a big part of the story Nehemiah just summarized: redemption is God's plan for His people.

As the leaders recognized what was happening, they decided to share their plan with the people. Confession is good for the *soul*, they say, but repentance is good for *everyone*. All people commit sins of commission or omission—violating God's will or ignoring it or choosing not to live by it—but it is changing course that brings us back into relationship with God. Repentance means you will no longer live in that sin or life of rebellion from God. The life-change, or course correction, aspect to sin transforms sin into a moment God can use to deepen our faith and impact real change with our renewed focus.

Imagine someone who has a problem with alcohol, or the more readily acceptable vice of overeating. Their sin is one of gluttony— over-consumption. Both *drugs* of choice lead to unhealth and long-term health consequences, but they are also forms of rebellion against God. They are a means to say, *God is not enough for me. I have to have this or that to be happy...and I have to have a lot of it!*

When a hangover from alcohol or food happens that next day, it is like the body is punishing us for bad choices. That feeling does not last too long because God did such an amazing job knitting our bodies together. Feeling bad that next morning normally lessens as the day goes on. The level of contrition and sadness starts to pass, and we move on. We may say *I'm sorry* (while meaning it) and make empty promises about learning our lesson and *never again* doing what we did. Those words are never enough, because there is no action.

I had a season in my life where I embraced alcohol as a way to move my focus from my unhappiness. I tasted alcohol, and I realized it made me feel good. The more I drank, the better I felt, and I wanted lots of it—the more the better, right?! I liked the way I felt and how care-free it made me feel. Alcohol is a drug that disconnects you from reality, and I was ready to think less about dissatisfaction with who I was and what I was doing.

I could *hold my liquor* as they say, which means I could drink excessively and not lose complete control. But these brief escapes from reality were only hurting me and my mind as the pain would set in the next day, residuals from the brain damage from the night before. It was only when I started to rehydrate desperately with water early on Sunday morning before I went to sleep, so I could make it to church later that day, that I knew I had to change.

To get over addictions, there must be change. Often the change has to be at a factor two times greater than the time spent in the struggle. If you have been over-consuming for some time, the change has got to be extreme enough to really get your attention. You may have to remove all of the alcohol from your house. If a certain food is your weakness...like say a certain product that came from the Garden of Eden...and comes seasonally. I don't know... like maybe a product that had the perfect amount of salty, peanut buttery goodness to balance with a covering of sweet milk chocolate, taking the form of...I don't know...Christmas trees, Valentine hearts, Easter eggs, and Halloween pumpkins...and I'm just spitballing here...you might not want to buy bags of that product. In fact, you may need to walk by them looking in the opposite direction, ignoring them completely. Not that I have any experience with this *fictional* product. Anything that replaces God's position in our lives must be removed.

Nehemiah and the leaders came up with the idea of a pledge. It was to be a written contract (Neh. 9:38). This contract was to be a tangible way for people to move on…to move back to where they were supposed to be, next to God. They were sending a message to the world that God's people were back home and they were committed to living for God once again. The leaders would represent the entire nation, and they were all going to sign it. If that sounds familiar, it should.

I love historical fiction, which means I enjoy history itself if the story is engaging enough. Few events in history captivate my attention like the beginning of the United States of America. I have read books from McCollough's *John Adams* to Ellis' *Founding Brothers*. I love the stories recounted in those books, not only because of the drama but because of the tension. The U.S.A. experiment came so close to not getting off the ground, and that story still speaks to us today the same way Israel's exodus and arrival in the Promised Land encouraged the Jews of Nehemiah's day.

There is a great television series from AMC called "TURN: Washington's Spies," which was adapted from a book by a similar name, authored by Alexander Rose. I watched every episode! The story of our nation's founding is told in a sensational way and is based in the facts of the true story of a spy ring that impacted the Revolutionary War. I even took my family to the International Spy museum in Washington D.C. where we saw the exhibits and lived the spy story.

The war began with a letter that declared the desire to start a new nation, which was signed by the leaders to give it authority— the Declaration of Independence. General Washington started the spy ring that would help win the war, also with a letter hiring Mr. Nathaniel Sackett for $50 a month with a bulging budget of $500 to stop the well-developed British espionage program. Sackett gave his life to the cause during the war, but that letter still merits and earns attention today because of the gravity of that mission.

Sanballat and his cronies, nearby nations, and transplants living around Israel expected with the wall built and this assembly, there would be a letter going to Persia declaring their independence...a *declaration of independence.* Conversely, the leaders of Israel were preparing a *declaration of dependence*...of sorts. They signed a pledge to show the people and anyone else that God was in charge and they were committed to living for God. The Jewish people would live or die going forward completely dependent on God's provision.

Nehemiah and the priests all signed the pledge. The Levites signed. The heads of the families signed. They all signed their names on the document that was to be sealed and displayed, with the names of each signer recorded in the book Nehemiah. They signed the pledge only after all of the people, including Nehemiah and the leaders, promised to follow all of the commandments in The Revelation of God—The Law.

To be clear about their "binding oath": it was to follow the Law as God explained it to Moses. Specifically, they promised to abide by the rules God had for His people and their relationship with Him. They vowed to not marry their children to foreigners or to abide by their practices on the Sabbath, which allowed for commerce and other activities. They would allow the land to rest from farming every seven years and to forgive debts that year. They agreed to pay the annual temple tax, which funded the regular maintenance of the Temple and the offerings to God: bread, grain, and whole-burnt (animals)—regular days, Sabbath, New Moons, Dedication, Absolution (atonement), and appointed feasts. All of the people—Levites, priests, and regular citizens—cast lots to determine who would provide the wood throughout the year for the Temple sacrifices as laid out by the Law from Moses.

All of that was about Israel's obligation to God: it was how they did what was required by God to worship Him properly…to bring God glory…to live daily for God. Next, they made a promise about their individual relationships with God. They would bring their first fruits from their crops and orchards, their firstborn sons and cattle as offerings to God. They would also care for the priests (and their families) who serve the Temple of God (the clergy) by providing them with the first born of their flocks. They vowed to fill the temple treasuries with the best of their grain, wine, oil, and fruit from their trees. They also vowed to maintain the care of the Levites who live in each of their towns as God appointed them. The people would bring their tithes (10% of income) to the Levites. They would also ensure a priest descended from Moses' brother, Aaron, would supervise the Levites, and the Levites would send a tithe to the Temple treasury from the tithe they received. They swore not to neglect the Temple of God and the worship that was to happen there.

The people of Israel—God's people—were now fully aware of what was required of them. The Law had been read to them and interpreted for them by their clergy—the Levites and priests. From the elite to the poorest of the poor, the rules apply to them, and so do the promises of safety and prosperity. They were ready. They all vowed to live for God and do what He told them to do. They had the foundation for a nation, and now they had to build on what God had given them.

God made a promise when King Solomon dedicated the first Temple. God knew His people would struggle, but God said if "My people who are called by My name humble themselves and pray and seek My face and turn from their wicked ways, then I will hear from heaven, will forgive their sin and will heal their land" (2 Chron. 7:14, NASB). God was faithful and ready to heal His people, and we will see in the next chapter that we must remain faithful as well.

CHAPTER 10

WHO'S WITH ME?!

WE HAVE SEEN SEVERAL examples mentioned earlier about the wholeness God intends for us—how our health is important to God, inside and out. Human beings were created to be in relationship with each other, and we are designed in a similar way with all of our systems in a symbiotic relationship. The physical—more tangible and apparent part of us—is no more or less important to health than the spiritual and mental realms. To put it frankly: our innards need attention too.

While being credited with the Gospel of John, the disciple Jesus loved also wrote some letters to encourage other followers of Jesus. In 3 John—the third letter in a series—John gives us insight that affirms God's plan for us. He is writing this letter to Gaius who is a fellow believer with some issues. Gaius isn't a name you hear anymore, but it is pronounced like Guy-us. It may help to read it as Guy or G, whatever works for you so you don't miss this point. John writes to Guy about loving and caring for strangers, empowering other followers of Jesus, and not returning evil for evil in his dealings with other leaders and disciples.

Before John begins his instructions to Gaius, he starts his letter how most of us do…with a greeting. In John's greeting he also gives Gaius a blessing, but it is the manner of blessing that I love. John wishes him well, but he does more than that. John says, "Beloved, I pray that in all respects you may prosper and be in good health, just as your soul prospers" (3 John 1:2, NASB). John knows Gaius. He found him, introduced him to Jesus, and he is overseeing that relationship to encourage him in his growth as a follower of Jesus.

Everything begins and ends with our relationship with Jesus—our spiritual health. John says, *I know your soul is doing well, but I want more for you.* John prays for Gaius to prosper in everything he does. We can see this as his mental toughness and intellect and ability. These are the very things which help us prosper in this life. John also addresses our third area in his blessing—Guy's physical health. John wants Guy to be in good shape…to be well…healthy and strong physically. John prays a blessing over Guy that he is connected to Jesus and for him to be healthy and prosperous. John prays for the outside to match the inside.

Jerusalem was secured with a wall. The external identity of the city was defined, but inside the walls, there was a problem—they had no identity or real composition. The temple was rebuilt and ready for the daily function of God's house. Ezra and the priests were in position to lead the religious life of the Temple. Nehemiah and the leaders were in Jerusalem, governing and leading the people to their future, but one more slight detail needed addressing: people.

The overwhelming majority of the people lived outside the walls of Jerusalem: Israelites, priests, Levites, Temple staff, and descendants of Solomon's slaves (Neh. 11:3). That needed to change. The people didn't live outside of Jerusalem because they didn't honor God or desire to live there; it wasn't safe. It was in ruins, and that was a constant reminder of defeat and destruction and shame. More people were required in Jerusalem to restore the life of that great city. People would have to pick up everything and leave their hometown to move to Jerusalem—a home they never knew. People were needed to populate the city, and Nehemiah came up with a plan.

Nehemiah's plan was to give people the *opportunity* to move… or to borrow from Don Corleone in *The Godfather* when he influenced a Hollywood mogul to cast one of his *godchildren* in a movie: "I'm gonna make *them* an offer *they* can't refuse." One out of ten people needed to move to Jerusalem. They drew lots to *get* to be volunteers. One out of ten people was drawn, and one out of ten people moved (Neh. 11:1). They dropped everything to move into Jerusalem and help restore God's plan for His people. Nehemiah didn't even have to cut off the head of a horse to get them to do what he needed, unlike Don Corleone. Moving to the big city may not sound like much of a grand gesture, but think about what that meant.[46]

I am from South Georgia; Savannah to be exact. If the governor came to me and said, *I know you like it in Savannah, but we need you to move to Atlanta to help start a new initiative to revive the city's downtown.* I don't know how excited I would be to be eligible for that *opportunity*. Of course, if it had been someone like Rev. Dr. Martin Luther King, Jr., or President John Adams—people I look up to—I might have been a little more excited about the prospect. God's people responded when Nehemiah asked them to move, and Nehemiah kept a record of who was serving God.

Nehemiah lists with great detail who was leading Israel at that moment, and their genealogy was listed for any doubters, substantiating his facts. The legitimate Israelites who lived in the area were from two tribes—Judah and Benjamin—as the other ten tribes were forever lost after the Assyrian destruction and exile. From Judah's son Perez, there were 468 *valiant* men. From the family of

Benjamin, 928 men lived in Jerusalem including the mayor of the city, Joel, and second in command, Judah. Representing the priests, 822 men worked in the Temple with an additional 242 men who were heads of families, and 128 strong warriors worked on security detail. The Levites had an additional 284 men plus 172 security guards who watched the gates (Neh. 11:4-19).

Nehemiah developed the infrastructure, and he listed the family leadership and those who managed the Temple staff, who led the singers for worship, and the legal advocates for the people at the royal court. Next, he listed the towns and suburbs of Judah where the people lived outside the walls of Jerusalem. Lastly, Nehemiah details the towns and suburbs of Benjamin. The descendants of Judah and Benjamin filled the reconstituted nation and their towns were recorded as a base for who the people of Israel were.

To ensure God's Law—the Revelation of God to Moses—Nehemiah continued the registry of the nation of Israel. God had brought His people home, but Nehemiah wanted to be crystal clear about *who* God's people were. That meant Nehemiah had to do more record-keeping and research, and he had to track down more names.

Nehemiah catalogued the names of every priest and Levite who came back with Zerubbabel during the earlier migration (Neh. 12:1). Their detailed records were due in part to the Persian king Darius who registered everyone. The wall was built, Temple worship was restored, the people had renewed the covenant with God, and now it was time to celebrate God's great work.

God has given us the means to be healthy, but we have to do our part. *Exerceo Divina* is successful because it engages God in a different way than we are used to finding God. We tend to separate our physical training from our spiritual health, but God does not work that way. God is relational, and He created us to be relational, not only in practice but also in the composition and functionality of our bodies.

The most appropriate language for connecting the three parts of our essence as human beings in one activity does not come from me. Wallace J. Nichols describes the essential element for us to connect our body, mind, and soul in his work, <u>Blue Mind</u>. His text looks at the science around the benefits of our proximity to water, and he uses science to show how water makes us "happier, healthier, more connected, and better at what you do." Yes, please! Nichols uses the term "flow" to describe the amazing way our body's three systems coexist in an almost magical way. Before I get to *flow*, I need to look at a foundational concept first.

Based on a great deal of research, Nichols suggests when our brain is resting it is not really resting at all but recharging and functioning in a way it cannot when we are focusing on a task. He heard M. A. Greenstein speak at a Blue Mind conference, describing this rest-but-not-at-rest status as our "default-mode network," also known as "drift." Greenstein says, "Drift is the freedom to wander in consciousness, and it's quite possibly one of the most important keys to the actual functioning of our nervous system."[47] We are task-driven people. We focus on a job and try to get it done. Scientists are teaching us that even though it is counter-intuitive, our brains are more efficient and effective when we are NOT focusing on a task. As Greenstein says, this is one of the MOST important keys to our nervous system working properly. Daydreamers around the world would be doing cartwheels right now if they weren't staring out the window.

When we are in *drift* mode, our brains consume large amounts of glucose for energy and a significant level of oxygen.[48] The theory holds that the default-mode network uses all of that energy and oxygen to organize our experiences, make connections, and prepare for future situations.[49] As Albert Einstein suggests, "Creativity is the residue of wasted time."[50] Our *drift* time engages the hippocampus area of the brain, which is in charge of creating new memories and new learning. This understanding explains why we often solve a problem doing something that has nothing to do with that situation. Unfortunately for us, we can't just stare out the window when we want to solve a problem, but the answer is on the other side of that glass.

Nichols explains that the best way to allow your brain to make those connections and create is what he calls "flow." While Nichols believes the best medium for flow is being in, on, or under the water, the idea is similar to a *runner's high*. Nichols explains there are four requirements to experience flow, and I believe they are essential to improving our health by encountering and experiencing God.

The first condition is the activity should be something you enjoy, which helps with the next step. The second condition is the activity must be something at which you have achieved some level of capability. This means you are good enough at the activity that you do not have to focus so much on actually *doing* it. The third condition is crucial to flow: the activity has to present a challenge of some kind. You need to be tested by difficulty, speed, technical trails, or something that pushes you. The final condition required for *flow* is you lose track of time.[51] I summarize the four conditions this way: (1.) Something you enjoy. (2.) Something you are good at. (3.) Something that challenges you. (4.) Something that frees you from the constraints of time.

Exerceo Divina is successful because of *flow*. All four of those conditions are a part of the program, but when we look a little deeper, we realize time-tested *Lectio Divina* relies on those conditions as well. As a reminder, *Lectio Divina* involved reading a passage from the Bible, meditating on that passage, praying to God about what God is saying in that passage, and contemplating where God is leading you in the passage. We merge *flow* and *Lectio Divina* this way: We enjoy reading God's Word—the Bible; we think and muse and speculate—something we do a great deal; we pray to God about what we are hearing in the passage—what is a challenge for us; and we contemplate God which frees us from space and time. In this practice and effort, we find *flow* and draw near to God. Life is not drudgery, and engaging God in all aspects of our lives leads to transformation.

The wall around Jerusalem had been completed. It was built. The gates were hung and working properly. Life was getting back to what most people knew to be normal. The wall needed to be dedicated to God's purposes. It was a wall composed of stone, earth, and baked bricks, but God was the most important ingredient in its composition. God was leading the rebuilding effort, working through Nehemiah as he responded and organized the people. They were ready to restart the nation, and Nehemiah had tirelessly worked to determine who was with God and who was on the outside looking in. With the massive wall effort complete, it was time for a celebration.

The Levites worked "exuberantly" on the dedication, writing "thanksgiving hymns" and songs that included the playing of cymbals, harps, and lutes (Neh. 12:27, MSG). Holy singers came from the villages all around Jerusalem. The priests and Levites followed the provision in the Law for purification, purifying themselves, the people, the wall, and the gates. They would all be ceremonially clean, and they did it all while wearing smiles on their faces with joy in their hearts.

I graduated from the U.S. Naval Academy years ago, but I will never forget Induction Day (I-Day). One of the first things you have to memorize is the Mission of the U.S. Naval Academy. The first phrase of that mission is: "To develop Midshipmen morally, mentally, and physically." During plebe year—freshmen year— life is not pleasant. That is a nicer way of saying I wished I was somewhere else…anywhere else. They sum up the Naval Academy this way: "They take away your God-given rights and give them back to you one at a time as privileges." Truer words have never been spoken.

I did not come by happiness easily that year. Some of you right now are having a hard time finding happiness as well, but we need to be concerned with our mental health. When you are having a hard time, you need to find a path to happiness. I came across the video of a woman who figured out the path to happiness: simple pleasures.

Candace Payne is a mom in Texas, and she used Facebook Live to post a video she shot in her car. She became known as the "Chewbacca mask woman." She went to Kohl's Department Store to buy yoga pants, but she bought a mask for herself, admitting her children were going to steal her mask, but she clarified the mask was for her enjoyment. The *Star Wars* franchise Chewbacca mask she bought has a strap that goes over the top of your head to hold it in place while your chin rest on the bottom of the mask. When you open your mouth, the mask mouth opens and the iconic Chewbacca roar erupts from a speaker on the mask.

The video shows Payne excitedly opening the box, building the excitement to reveal her unknown purchase to viewers. With the mask on her face, she laughs hysterically, seeing herself on her phone and hearing the sounds coming from her face. She cannot stop laughing, which means Chewbacca just keeps on roaring. It really is funny, and it is hard not to laugh. The video went viral. She posted the video in May 19, 2016, and she has over 150M views.[52] Because of the video's popularity, Payne has received nearly $500,000 in gifts and cash from Kohl's, made talkshow appearances, and received a Disney World vacation, including $400,000 worth of scholarship money for her two young children to Southeastern University in Lakeland, FL. The popularity of Payne's video tells us people really need a good laugh.

Our happiness and perspective are often colored by how the world sees us. Instead of seeing ourselves the way God does: beloved children with great potential and hope. We see ourselves through the eyes of others as we project our unhappiness onto them. We perceive negativity that may not actually be there, and we focus on what we do not have. We believe others were hyper-sensitive to every step we take, every decision we make, and every leaf in our yard we do not rake. It is as if we have fallen so in love with *reality TV* that we think we are on a show, but no one is filming or actually watching.

Why do we get so focused on ourselves? When we serve our own pursuits instead of God's plan, we are going to struggle, and happiness will be difficult to find. The Levites were finding their happiness in God and God's plan. They were overwhelmed with joy about what God had done and was doing through the rebuilding of the wall and Jerusalem, and they relished the opportunity to be involved in that plan.

Nehemiah left no stone unturned. Alright. That is a bad pun about building the wall, but it seemed appropriate. He was a man of details, and he did not leave anything open to failure or criticism. He knew how important perception was, and he did not want to give ammunition to anyone to possibly tear down the work God was doing for Israel.

Nehemiah had two choirs prepare for the big day (Neh. 12:31). After much practicing, they were ready. Both choirs followed the leaders of Judah up onto the wall. One choir went to the right toward the Refuse Gate. Some of the younger priests played their trumpets. Ezra, the priest and scholar, led the bulk of the choir playing the instruments of King David. They paraded around the city on the wall.

The second choir proceeded in the opposite direction around the city, marching on the wall. Nehemiah and half the crowd followed them. They walked over the Tower of Furnaces to the Broad Wall, over the Ephraim Gate, the Jeshanah Gate, the Fish Gate, the Tower of Hananel, and the Tower of a Hundred, past the Sheep Gate. They stopped at the Prison Gate.

The two choirs arrived at the Temple of God. The trumpets played. The singers sang. The Temple of God vibrated with the sound of praise as God was glorified and celebrated as He should be honored. All who gathered there—leaders, priests, Levites, and the people of God—praised God with great emotion and joy. Women and children sang right along with the choirs, making a wonderful sound. Sacrifices were offered such that the air in and around Jerusalem smelled like barbecue and grilling on an afternoon in the South at a college football game. God was glorified for what He had done!

As the Temple system came into operation, there were some more details to address about the logistics that were required. Someone had to collect the offerings and then handle the accounting side of fund management. They had to ensure the funds were disseminated to the correct accounts. This type of work is not always intriguing, but it is essential.

In the Navy Supply system, these appointed positions would be Storekeepers (SKs)—stock control specialists, and I worked with many of them over my years of military service. The role of the *beancounter* can be a thankless job, but they are vital to ensuring supplies are where they are supposed to be when they are needed. The Temple SKs were responsible for the storerooms and proper fund management to sustain the priests and Levites. The Temple funds provided for their housing and food—room and board, and every shekel was to be accounted for.

God's people were overwhelmed with the job the priests, Levites, singers, and security guards were doing. They learned what it looked like to praise God and feel God through their worship. They wanted to repay those Temple employees for the job they were doing, and they also were honoring what God revealed in The Revelation. The priests, Levites, and others were doing their job, and the people wanted to fulfill their responsibilities as well. Nehemiah made sure they did what they promised, paying the allowances and providing the dedicated goods to the Temple staff. And the Israelites were overjoyed to do their part once again.

The wall was secure, and the city was starting to thrive again. Inside and outside of Jerusalem, Nehemiah's plan was working, but we should never rest on our laurels—trusting too much in our own success. In the next chapter, we see why goals have to be revisited sometimes.

CHAPTER 11

BEST LAID PLANS

A MAN IS PLOWING HIS field. It was time to clear obstacles to growth and productivity out of the way. He had done this very thing before, and he knew he would do it again. The man had worked this field for years without incident, except that this field had provided food for him and his family. It was time to plow, and he was ready and willing to do his job.

As the man labored in the field, preparing to do what was needed for a future crop and sustenance, something happened. It had never happened to him before, and we know this because of his reaction. He is shaken by the event, and it causes him to stop what he is doing for an existential moment.

The man working his field plowed through a mouse's nest, destroying it. Of course, this story is relayed to us by Robert Burns in the poem "To a Mouse," which was published in 1785. Burns gives us a great line from this poem that has more than once applied to me: "The best laid schemes o' Mice an' Men Gang aft agley, An' lea'e us nought but grief an' pain, For promis'd joy!"[53] My version: The best laid plans of mice and men often go awry, and we are left with grief and pain where joy had been promised.

The man is saddened by his role as the destroyer of the mouse' home with winter just weeks away. He regrets violating the *live and let live* bond with his mortal neighbor. He laments the troubles that come from regretting the past and making plans for the future that never transpire—destroying the mouse's home and thinking he would plow without incident. He goes so far as expressing jealousy of the mouse because he does not regret past mistakes or try to see into the future—the mouse only knows the present—and this seems like a better option than is current predicament. Our best laid plans sometimes go awry. Even with the right focus and effort, we can get off God's path.

Nehemiah developed a system. The wall was rebuilt, and the Temple was functioning. The people moved back into Jerusalem, and they had been taught what God expected of them. God's plan was working, but doing what is required is never as easy as we want it to be.

The exploration of God's Law continued for some time as people tried to understand what their history was. God had given Israel the blueprints on how to keep their end of the covenant, and they were now rediscovering the plans. Worship was one thing, but trying to live out their faith was definitely another.

As the Law was read and enforced, something became clear rather quickly: God had a particular way of doing everything. The Moabites and Ammonites had been interspersed throughout the nation for some time. They were neighbors: Moab to the east of the Jordan and Ammon just north of Moab. They were not part of God's plan, and they were not to be confused with His chosen people. In fact, those two nations were around for a thousand years before they were absorbed into the Babylonian and Persian empires. They were not good neighbors to Israel, and God does not forget.

When the Israelites were on their journey to the Promised Land, they were not ready to claim the land. Israel was a new nation, and they had not fully realized their identity came from God and not through the usual political, government-based plan that was the norm in the world. As they journeyed up from Egypt by way of the desert wilderness of Sinai into Canaan, there were many groups of foreigners and smaller nations. Moab and Ammon were mentioned in that part of Israel's story, for not letting them take a shortcut through their sovereign lands. They refused to provide them with food or water, and their leaders even hired Balaam, a magician/shaman, to curse Israel and foretell their destruction by influencing the gods. The best laid plans… God took the intended curse and made it a blessing on Israel, and Moab and Ammon were forever marked by the curse that came back on them.

The Ammonites and Moabites had become part of the society over the years as the Law was ignored, nations began to push Israel around, and God stopped honoring His part of the covenant because the Israelites had rejected Him. Little by little, the differences between Israel and Moab and Ammon disappeared for the sake of commerce and community. That changed the day the Law was read, they understood God's plan, and they committed to follow God as a nation again. All of the Moabites and Ammonites were sent out of Israel that day, and more disciplinary actions and difficult decisions were to follow.

With the rejuvenation of the people and their recommitment to God, things seemed to be going really well. Life was good in Israel as people honored God again, and they began to see a new future. As the story of Israel teaches us and as many followers of Jesus know, complacency is one of the Devil's favorite tools.

Nehemiah had to return to King Artaxerxes (Neh. 13:6). He was his employee, and he had been summoned by the king. Nehemiah was under royal appointment. He was the governor of the Judean region—what was once Judah. Nehemiah had done everything he intended to do. The Temple operations had been restored, the wall was rebuilt and functioning, and the people were honoring God and returning their tribute to the conquering King Artaxerxes. Nehemiah went back to Babylonia with confidence and a sense of accomplishment for all that God had done through him and for him.

The people of Israel were no different than us. Many people get convicted by a sermon during a Sunday morning worship service, and they may even swear they will change their ways. It may happen on Friday night or it may happen on Monday morning, but backsliding is part of many a faith walk. With the best of intentions, we make promises, and we may try really hard. But like the commanding officer of the aircraft carrier in the movie "Top Gun," we are "writing checks *our* butts can't cash." None of us can make promises to change, if we do not let Jesus do the changing. The Israelites were no different.

For clarity and peace in our lives, we need to have goals. I recommend a basketball goal. There is something quite simplistic about basketball. While football and baseball have nuance, basketball does not, fundamentally.

Football has offensive and defensive coordinators who coach eleven players on either side of the ball on the field for each play that is run. They speak a different language, and even sports commentators do not know what is being communicated. They often have coaches or quarterbacks on their radio and television shows, and the hosts ask the experts to call a *normal* pass or run play.

These plays consist of a quarterback to throw the ball to a receiver with everyone having an assigned task or a run play that details who gets the ball, where they need to run, and what everybody else has to do to make that happen.

They do not use bottle tops and pebbles to show people the play in the huddle like many people did growing up in neighborhood football games. Chris Sims, who played college and professional football as a quarterback—the ones who had to call the play—met with Stu Woo, a "Wall Street Journal" sports reporter to discuss play-calling. Sims gave a *normal* play: "West right slot. 72. 'Z' Bingo. 'U' Split. Can it with 58 Lexus. Apple 314 Hammer… Dummy snap count on 1." Formation. Protection. Route Concept. Snap Count. Sims said, on a regular game week, he would have to know 200-225 plays and, of course, be able to call the play in the huddle.[54] That sounds difficult, because it is.

Contrary to what Durham Bulls Manager Joe Riggins in the movie "Bull Durham" says, baseball is no easier. In an iconic scene, Riggins orders the entire baseball team into the showers to chew them out. After throwing ten baseball bats onto the floor of the shower room, he says, "This is a simple game. You throw the ball. You hit the ball. You catch the ball." True, but that overly simplifies a game that has become even more technical in the last decade with Sabermetrics, analytics, and quantitative analysis, using statistics to decide who gets to play and in what scenarios they should play.

Every swing of the bat—missed ball, foul tip, or hit—gets tracked; as does every pitch. Managers make decisions based on hard data, sometimes ignoring *gut* feelings and players on a streak. The Houston Astros even got in a great deal of trouble by Major League Baseball (MLB) for a sign-stealing scandal in 2017 and 2018. Their illegal system utilized a camera, a television, and a trash can to signal certain pitches were about to be thrown. The team won the 2017 World Series, and the Astros were crowned world champions. Now, their achievement will forever be tainted and a permanent scar on the game of baseball. In the wake of the scandal, the General Manager and manager were fired, the team lost draft picks, and they had to pay a $5M fine to MLB. Yeah… This is a simple game?!

In the game of basketball, the court is 94 feet by 50 feet. There are two rims with nets 10 feet above the floor, with backboards on either end of the court. Teams move toward their goal to score points, and they move back to defend and stop the other team from scoring points on their goal. The ball either goes through the rim and net to score points…or…it doesn't. Hall of Famer Reggie Miller put it this way in an interview with Dan Patrick in 2019: "Everybody pretty much runs the same plays, you just try and stop the other team. Everyone knows what you are going to do." The game is there before you, and you try to execute better than your opponent. Simple.

The simplicity of basketball is why you see so many goals at the end of driveways as you drive around your town. With a ball and a goal, you can play basketball for hours, whether by yourself or with anyone who shows up. Playing a basketball game is straight forward, putting a basketball goal together is another story, and I have a story I do not share easily.

I had a goal not too long ago; it was Christmas 2019. My daughter wanted a basketball goal from Santa Claus, and she does not ask for much, if anything, which I love. So, when she wanted that, my wife and I had to make it happen. They play basketball at their elementary school during P.E., and we knew both kids would enjoy a basketball goal. I know I did as a kid. It was always there when I needed to step outside into the cold or heat, and just spend some time by myself. I spent many hours shooting baskets, and I knew the kids would love it, too.

The *Santa* part of this plan was the hard part. How to build a basketball goal and not be noticed by the children was harder than I imagined. My plan: open the enormous box that barely fit into the bed of my Chevy Traverse, take all of the parts into the attic, assemble the goal in sections, and then on Christmas Eve connect everything together. Simple. Yeah… West right slot. 72. 'Z' Bingo. 'U' Split. Can it with 58 Lexus. Apple 314 Hammer…Dummy snap count on 1…kind of simple…except I was the dummy in this story.

I got everything into the attic without issue. I am nothing if not determined, even when stupidity starts to creep into the picture. The lighting in the attic is bad, and I was having to work at night. I put the base together and I put two pieces of the three sections for the backboard support pole. When I added the third section, unknowingly I did not match up the pole correctly. As I banged the third section on, it was really, really hard. I did not know I was doing it wrong, and I was slamming the pole pieces together per the instructions by lifting the united pieces straight up to the roof (which I could only do in one area of the attic because of the pitch of the roof) and slamming it into the third piece. It was like trying to put a fat foot in a small shoe. You know it does not fit, but you want to see what it looks like on your foot to really know. Again…stupid.

Not one to give up….ever…I got those pieces together. Everything was staged and ready for several days later when Christmas Eve would provide the time and cover of darkness to assemble the goal in the garage and driveway. At this point, I thought my plan was working.

After church and supper at home, the kids went to bed and I went to work. I lowered everything from the attic into the garage by myself. More stupid time as that stuff was really heavy and could have dragged me to my death, falling down the ladder. I could just see the headline now: "Pastor Dies Proving There Is a Santa Claus." It was not the way I wanted to go out, but I survived the ladder exercise. The worst was yet to come.

With my car in the driveway and out of the garage, I got back into the directions and start assembling. It was not long before I realized I had a problem…a BIG problem. As I started to assemble the adjustable height bar, I realized the fatal flaw: the third section of the pole was facing the wrong direction: it was 45 degrees off center. There was no fixing this. As snug as that fat foot was in those trendy shoes after a day on your feet in the South Georgia heat, the piece would not come out. I even bothered our neighbor at 11 p.m. on Christmas Eve…CHRISTMAS EVE…to come help me. Nothing says let's celebrate the birth of the Savior of the world like trying to pull sections of a pole apart that might as well have been welded together. We couldn't do it. Stupidness took a break here before we tried using his truck, my Traverse, and chains to pull it apart. I finally acknowledged this was not going to work. I failed miserably. It was time for a new plan.

Our plan…let's come up with a good lie about Santa, and live to fight another day. We put the pieces in the corner of the garage. I wrote a letter in my best non-Daddy handwriting. (I did an epic job here. You would have thought I had been trained by the CIA to hide my identity. This part went well.) I explained how the goal got damaged in route to their house, and Daddy was going to take it to Academy Sports + Outdoors and exchange it there. In fact, this is what Daddy did, and I assembled the goal in the sunlight in the driveway on December 26th…no mistakes this time.

Mistakes happen. Challenges happen. We cannot control everything—that is why they call them accidents—but we can control how we react and respond. We need to stop *stupid* before it takes control and makes things worse. You and I need to know when what we are doing is NOT working, and we need to figure out a new plan. An intervention goes a long way to getting us back in God's good graces.

In the 32nd year of Artaxerses, while Nehemiah was away… traveling through the fertile crescent…up to Mesopotamia and down to Persia…the backward migration of Abraham from Ur of the Chaldeans to Canaan over a thousand years earlier…things got dicey back home. One of the priests (Eliashib to be specific) decided to break the rules for a less than upstanding individual. It was the compromised and dishonest politician Tobiah. We do not know what Eliashib owed him or what he was hoping to get in return, but he let Tobiah have access to a Temple storeroom. As Forrest Gump famously recited words from his mama: "Stupid is as stupid does." Why would Eliashib rent out a Temple storeroom? you ask, because he probably thought he could get away with it.

It was a large storeroom, and it was God's pantry…GOD. The grain-offerings, incense, and worship vessels to honor God were kept in there. Along with those holy items, the tithe offerings—holy parts of God's worship plan—were stored there. This included the grain, wine, and oil given from the people for the musicians, security guards, and Levites as well as the offerings intended for the priests. This was a holy space in the most holy place in Israel, and Eliashib gave a key to a politician…and a corrupt one at that. Not good.

Nehemiah was gone a long time: probably months of travel and time in country. There would have been meetings with the king and debriefs about how things had gone and were going. It would have been very important for Nehemiah to assure the king of his and Israel's intention to continue in their vassal role, keeping their end of the covenant with Persia and paying their protection money. Nobody with any real understanding of their situation would deem the Jewish people a threat at this time, because they simply were not ready to fight off a marauding band of militia, nor the super power of the day.

Nehemiah knew why he had gone back to Babylon. It was a political mission. He was going to have to play the games again at the highest level where he learned many years ago, in that same royal court. How could he say enough without saying too much? How could he give enough respect but not seem undignified? How could he be true to God's authority without offending the king and nation that owned Israel? Nehemiah entered a minefield, but God was with him. He completed his tasks, and he began the journey home...back to Jerusalem.

After a successful trip to Babylon, Nehemiah was greeted with the normal how-do-you-dos. People were glad to have him back home. Nehemiah was missed, but the damage of what was done in his absence had to be addressed. I can imagine the relief Nehemiah had felt when he finally walked back into the governor's house. He puts his bags down and starts putting things away. He checks his calendar for tomorrow and the coming days. As he goes to relax for a moment before a brisk walk around Jerusalem to check on things, he grabs the latest issue of "Jerusalem Jabber," the rumor rag and celebrity gossip journal of the day. I can see the article lead:

"Temple room for rent…just contact Eliashib the priest…" How quickly do you think Nehemiah shot out of his house?!

Off to the Temple he flew. Nehemiah was not half-cocked, he was fully cocked…locked and loaded. I would not have wanted to be Eliashib that day. Nehemiah was angry…very angry! He was irate, and he was going to fix the problem. He did not even address the priests. He found the room in question, and he took every last piece of Tobiah's junk out of the storeroom. He did not just move it and politely restack it in the hallway. No. How did he get his point across? Nehemiah dumped all of Tobiah's gear in the street (Neh. 13:8). Message sent. But there was more to do.

Nehemiah had the priests ceremonially cleanse the room. But first, he had them take all of the worship vessels and grain-offerings that were housed in there out of the room. Once it was clean again, he directed them to get the room in order, filling it back up with the intended supplies and offerings. Unfortunately, this was only the beginning of the infractions he would have to address.

The Temple workers had daily responsibilities. There were numerous sacrifices and requirements by the Law. Cleanliness was important, and the butchering of animals for sacrifices was extensive. Worship also involved significant work with musicians and singers. The priests and Levites had much to do to maintain the worship of God. Just as there was a detailed plan for the worship of God, there was exacting detail for how the priests would be paid and on what they would subsist. The balance of donations and offerings had to be honored. Unfortunately, the people were not honoring their commitment.

Nehemiah came home to find many of the Temple staff had left Jerusalem, returning to their homes not out of rebellion but out of necessity. The people had stopped bringing their offerings.

The Levites ran out of food and had no way to survive. They kept at their work until they realized they were going to starve. They went home to start working the land and animals to provide for themselves and their families.

Nehemiah called the leadership to a meeting, and then he ripped into them for not doing their jobs. He started cleaning house. He made difficult decisions…and maybe some easy ones. He removed multiple people who failed to do their jobs, Eliashib being one of them. Much like a parent who has been out of town and returns home early to find the children swinging from the ceiling fan and smashing glasses on the kitchen floor as a wild party swirled around them, Nehemiah let them have it. Whatever he said worked, and no one was going to second guess him that day.

While it was more like an empty theater on a Tuesday afternoon than the thriving household of God, all of the Temple personnel returned to their posts. Nehemiah restored worship and the Temple sacrifices, and the people saw it and smelled the sacrifices. In response, the people started showing up with their tithe offerings. They returned to their obligation by bringing ten percent of their grain, wine, and oil to the storerooms (Neh.13:12).

Nehemiah responded to the resurgence of giving by putting quality people of his choosing in charge of the storerooms. Nehemiah picked one representative from each section of the Temple personnel—three descendants of Levi to replace Eliashib. Shelemiah was picked from the priests. Zadok was selected from the scribes, and Pedaiah was chosen from the Levites. Nehemiah made sure they had everything they needed to succeed, including a qualified assistant to the three representatives named Hanan. All four of these men had impeccable reputations for honesty and hard work. Their job was to manage the supplies and storerooms, ensuring all of the priests, Levites, and scribes received their provisions and allotments. Nehemiah did everything he could to make sure what transpired while he was gone would not happen again. With those individuals appointed and prepared to do the job, Nehemiah prayed to God for His blessing and support to acknowledge and endorse all he was doing for God's plan of redemption.

While Nehemiah was the governor of Judah for King Artaxerses, he was serving a higher authority: God. He had to report to the king on a regular basis, but his work for God never stopped. Just as he addressed one issue or failing of the people, another would pop up. Prayer is what sustained him, and he would need God once again.

Nehemiah knew the story of Israel well, and he was not going to let them repeat the mistakes of the past...not on his watch. Just as God promised King Solomon to heal Israel when they returned to Him, God made a promise to him about what would happen if they turned from following God. God told King Solomon,

> But if you turn away and forsake My statutes and My commandments which I have set before you, and go and serve other gods and worship them, then I will uproot you from My land which I have given you, and this house which I have consecrated for My name I will cast out of My sight and I will make it a proverb and a byword among all peoples (2 Chron. 7:19-20, NASB).

The people of Israel had already forsaken God's Law and dealt with the consequences before, and Nehemiah was going to do everything he could to not let it happen again.

The Fourth Commandment described what God intended for the Sabbath: the people were supposed to rest from their labors. Resting was vital to God's plan. He wanted the people to rest. God used land management as a means to teach the people about rest.

The Law explained the land was to rest on the seventh year as the people allowed the land to replenish with the nutrients it required for more production. The year before the fallow year would provide enough harvest to sustain the seventh year. It was a matter of faith, and the people had to trust God to provide for them. In the same way, the people were to prepare enough food on the sixth day to rest on the Sabbath. They were not supposed to work on the seventh day.

One reason for this was to allow their bodies to rest. When they were slaves in Egypt that had been forced to work when told, and now they were being told to work hard, but rest was necessary. The second and more important reason to honor the Sabbath was because God told them to do that, and it was an obvious way for God and others to know if Israel belonged to God or not.

As Nehemiah settled back into life in Judah, he realized that people were not showing their allegiance to God; they were rejecting His Sabbath. Every Saturday—their Sabbath day—people were working, mainly in commerce and retail operations. Nehemiah watched people treading on wine presses to produce wine, carrying heavy loads of grain to sell in the market, and loading their donkeys with all sorts of goods to buy, sell, or exchange. They brought in wine, grapes, figs, and a whole list of items to fill the marketplace with choices.

People came from all over to make a buck, gaining some profit and feeding their families. Fishermen came from the Mediterranean coast from as far away as Tyre to sell their fish and selections from the sea, and residents loved the treasure trove of sea life and kept the fishermen coming back every week. Nehemiah stepped in and told them about the Law. He told the foreigners the Sabbath was God's day, and they needed to reconsider what they were doing because it violated God's covenant. This was the holy city of Jerusalem, and this practice of desecrating the Sabbath had to stop...right...now.

Nehemiah called the leaders of Judah together, including some of the merchants who owned the very business in question, and laid out the issue so there could be no confusion. *How quickly you forget*, he told the businessmen, continuing: *This is exactly how our people were destroyed by the Assyrians and exiled to Babylon. This exact infraction. God saved us from slavery and gave us our own land—a home for the first time. All He asked for was our allegiance. Only a short while ago, we rededicated our nation to God, and you have gone and done it again* (Neh. 13:17-18). The leaders were having what I call a *Britney Spears moment*.

Britney Spears got famous during the mid to late 1990s as a pop music recording artist. She won countless awards, but one of her first, if not biggest, hits was "Oops!... I Did It Again" about getting carried away with love. Unfortunately, she also got carried away with drugs and other issues in her life, and her career failed. The Spears' *Oops* syndrome is more about the song than anything else. It just means, I've made this exact mistake before, but I have not learned my lesson yet. The Israelites were having a *Britney Spears moment*.

Nehemiah, taking on the role of God's anointed, took charge once again. As Friday afternoon moved on, he had the city gates closed and locked. Nehemiah stationed trusted servants at every gate. No retail goods, food (produce or otherwise), or products were to be allowed to enter Jerusalem (Neh. 13:19). The gates would reopen on Saturday night…but no sooner.

Change is hard, and the merchants were unhappy. For several weeks, some merchants came and camped outside the gate with intentions to enter the city after hours and set up for the Sabbath market. Nehemiah was not having any of that, and he yelled out to them, you're trespassing, and if you stay out there, we will drive you off by force if necessary. *You don't have to go home, but you can't stay here.* That was the end of that. They got the point, and they stopped trying to sell their goods on the Sabbath. Old habits die hard, and new habits are not easily forged, but persistence does pay off.

I participated in a great way to build a habit during the Christmas holidays as part of the "Runner's World" running challenge. (I also started another version during the COVID shutdown.) Their plan was to run every day between Thanksgiving and New Year's Day. The minimum required to be classified as a *streaker* was running one mile per day. That's it. If you think about running every, single day for 30-something days, that number of days can seem too difficult to fathom. That's definitely what I thought.

I have run eight marathons, but I had never run more than three days per week in preparation for those races. Running every day seemed impossible, but I started my streak on Thanksgiving Day, November 28, 2019. I, of course, had to make it harder on myself as I determined to run two miles per day instead of one mile. My logic was one mile just seemed too short of an effort.

I ran day after day for 40 days, into 2020. In all, I ran 123.37 miles, averaging running a 5k (3.1miles) every day. I surprised myself, and I found myself looking forward to those daily running efforts. Besides the obvious benefits of helping maintain my weight during the holidays, the benefits to my mental health during a stressful season were also realized. I found out committing to a challenge is doable, and it only took my devotion one day at a time. It was about planning to be faithful for 40 days; my running challenge took place one day at a time.

Consistency makes strides that occasional success cannot. Nehemiah told those merchants he had set the policy, and it was not going to change. His last step in honoring the Sabbath was to make even his Sabbath policy congruent with the Sabbath law. He had stopped the illegal work on the Sabbath, but to do so, he made those trusted employees work on the Sabbath as security guards. To rectify that, he asked the Levites to make themselves ceremonial clean, so they could work the gate as part of the Temple worship preparations and procedures. Now, no one was doing unlawful work on God's day. Nehemiah had been threatened by many of the merchants and foreigners, but he came out on the other side, maintaining God's Law and still alive. He prayed to God giving thanks, and he asked to remain in God's favor as he continued to do his job as governor and God's man for his time.

Life went on in Judah, and their nation tried to serve God, but their leaders could not help themselves when it came to setting bad examples. Nehemiah had to show the people the way one more time. Much to Nehemiah's horror, he found out some Jews had rejected their renewed covenant by marrying women from other nations: Ashdod, Ammon, and Moab. It was another *Britney Spears moment.*

Nehemiah went to interview these men and their families. He found that half of the children of these illegal marriages could not speak *Hebrew.* That was all he could bare. Nehemiah tore into their hides, figuratively and literally. In Psalm 69:9, King David says, "For zeal for Your house has consumed me, and the reproaches of those who reproach You have fallen on me." Nehemiah was beyond reproach at this moment as he became a zealot for God.

Nehemiah scolded these men. He slapped them around good. He got so forceful that he pulled out some of their hair. He left the women and children alone, but he let those Jewish men know clearly that they were not allowed to continue this way. He made them promise…swear…to not marry members of other nations nor marry their own children to foreigners. To prove his point, he brought up the wisest king to ever live: Solomon. He reminded them of his downfall—foreign women…and lots of them. King Solomon married so many foreign women and allowed them to bring their many gods with them, he forgot who to worship and to whom he offered sacrifices. God fell into the divine caldron with every other false god in the pantheon of cultish deities; it was his downfall. This current evil did not stop with laymen, even priests had joined in this rebellion. The grandson of the high priest Eliashib had married a foreign woman. Nehemiah drove them all from his presence, and their violations did not go unnoticed by God or anyone else.

Nehemiah did everything in his power to cleanse the people of Israel and keep them from violating God's covenant. He maintained the Temple worship and ritual, and he did his job as governor to maintain the peace and justice throughout the land. Nehemiah closes his biblical account with a prayer that he prayed often. It is a prayer for us all as we desire to stand before God aligned with His will for our lives. It is a prayer about seeking God and doing what God requires. "Remember me, O my God, for good." May we all dwell in God's will, and no matter if we win or lose, our identity will be found in God, and it will be *good*.

Our story ends in a similar way to how it began: Nehemiah was a servant. He started off serving a foreign king, and he found his identity in service of the King of Heaven. Nehemiah was transformed, and now we need to follow his lead and we can reach the same destination.

The COVID pandemic of 2020 was certainly a time for change. Many people were forced to do things in a different way, and life was lived at a different pace. We all had to reprioritize our time and adjust to the changing norms of daily life. The experts said not to wear masks and to circulate in public in the midst of the early days of the pandemic, then we were told to isolate ourselves through shelter-at-home orders and social distancing. Wearing a mask became the new normal. We all learned about what change looks like.

When it comes to our health—physically, mentally, and spiritually—lasting change can involve resisting temptation, managing our finances and caring for people. James, the brother of Jesus, gives us the means to being physically, mentally, and spiritually healthier. In James 4, James teaches us how our troubles begin and are sustained.

His sage wisdom is similar to that of the movie version of the Swamp Fox: "Aim small, miss small." It is such a simple concept, but SO true. To make lasting change in any area of my life, I don't have to jump off a bridge. There are going to be habits we have to kick *cold turkey*, but it is best to think about change like the running challenge—one step at a time.

We want change to be grand and extravagant and showy because it FEELS like a big deal and that makes it more important.

So often, these grand gestures are not even for others as much as they are for ourselves. It makes us feel like the main character in *Anchorman: The Legend of Ron Burgundy* as he tries to impress a woman as he meets her: "I'm kind of a big deal. People know me. I'm very important. I have many leather-bound books…and…my apartment smells of rich mahogany." Yep, grand gestures make us feel just like that.[55]

We have this big chasm between where we need to be and where we actually are. To bridge that gap, it is obviously going to require a drastic change for us to get to where we need to be. Whether it is working on our mental health or education (continuing education, or learning a new skill) or physical health (exercising seven days per week, working out for hours per day, or losing 20 pounds as fast as possible), these are things we really need to do. But, should they merit some daunting transition?

James tells us a better approach is to check our motivation for our goals, which should be God's view of our health and not "Cosmopolitan" or "Men's Health" magazines. If I address this area of my life, will I see the benefits? Will I get healthier? Will I see results?! James was probably not writing about losing weight or eating a healthier/more sustainable diet, but those things are a part of discipleship—becoming like Jesus…being His follower. It is never enough to merely recognize the problem and NOT do anything to fix the problem.

James tells us: "But prove yourselves doers of the Word, and not merely hearers who delude themselves" (Neh. 1:22, NASB) James does not mince words, and I like that. Later in the letter, James says, we lust after the flesh, we are envious of what others have, we feel *less-than* around everyone else, and we ask God for the wrong things and with the wrong motives. James uses the words we see from Nehemiah, Hosea, and numerous other prophets: We are adulterers, forsaking God to give ourselves to the world (Neh. 4:4).

James tells us, God is jealous for our souls and He does not relent in His pursuit of us. God desires us, which is wonderful, but James tells us God is no pushover: "God is opposed to the proud, but gives grace to the humble" (Jas. 4:6b, NASB). Ruminate on that one for a bit. God opposes those that say they don't need Him or want any part of Him, which takes guts. Not only does it hurt God for us to reject Him and throw our arms around the Devil and his minions, but He then stands in opposition to us. Life is hard enough without having God work against your plans.

James follows up that newsflash with one of the best promises in the Bible: "Submit therefore to God. Resist the devil and he will flee from you. Draw near to God and He will draw near to you" (Jas. 4:7-8b, NASB). God means it! This is true…every time. Think about your own journey. I know God has never ignored my steps toward Him. It is important to remember this: God takes bigger steps than we do. If we take one step moving near God, He takes one step toward us as well. God closes the distance quicker than we do, and we will feel the warmth of His embrace and realize the nearness of His presence.

When we admit that we need God's help, He responds. When we call out to God, we are submitting to His plan and His provision. We draw near to God, and God draws near to us. Those words of promise are enough for us on this journey to health and our rebuilding process.

So, we come back to our dilemma: is the journey too much? Do we need a grand gesture? The journey is not too much for God. A promise. One step. Draw near. Move towards God. One step makes a big difference.

I was trained by the U.S. Marine Corps in land navigation. I learned how to navigate with a map and a compass at night or during the day. As we applied what we learned in extensive exercises and drills, I learned an important lesson: every little bit matters. Aim small, miss small. One degree change on the compass in land navigation results in 100ft of ground error per mile. That means for every 10° of error, you will be off your target by 1000ft. That distance is nearly two-tenths of a mile. We're talking 1000ft in the wrong direction.

The good news is, this same concept works when it come to corrective behavior as well—making a slight change works. If you are trying to quit smoking cigarettes, or indulging alcohol, drugs, or any type of addiction you can think of, we are not focusing on the full length of the journey. Remember, with focus and an honest assessment of where we are—either through the counsel of others or the voice of the Holy Spirit—we can make a substantial change. One degree change in our course, changes our destination by 100ft per mile.

During my running challenge, I ran 124 miles over 40 days. That one change—adding at least two miles of running per day to my schedule—had a big impact. Not only did I gain some much-needed confidence, but I ended up in a completely different location than I would have otherwise, figuratively. I changed course by one degree on my compass, and after 124 miles of running, I arrived over two miles away from where I would have ended up without the change.

Changing our lives to become healthier is incremental...one day...one step in the right direction. *Aim small, miss small.* Walking one hour per day at a 4mph pace burns 400 calories. That means without changing your diet, walking one hour per day will result in you losing one pound in nine days.

When I need to make a change, I have to begin with one clear target, however small it is. As long as I am improving my health, one area…one change is enough and is something upon which we can build. Our desire to change originates in our belief—our faith—that God IS saving us. God offers us salvation, saving us from sin. If we choose to follow Jesus, God begins making us new, and nothing is more powerful than He is.

You and I make a statement about God by whether or not we care enough to try. Nehemiah was in a position to do something for God that needed to be done. He could have chosen his own way and his own plans when he heard about the state of things in Jerusalem, but he chose to follow God. He had one conversation with the king, and he changed course. We know what is lacking and what our discrepancies are. Let's aim for one thing. One change. *Aim small, miss small.* Focus on one thing and be honest about how we are doing. With God's assistance and direction, we will be successful.

Eliminate one food from your diet. Walk. Run. Pray. Make a lasting change, one day at a time. Take one step nearer to God, and you will be amazed by what God can do. Nehemiah tells you and me: "Arise and build." The rebuilding effort begins right now…at this moment…in some area of our lives. With God's help, as we rebuild our lives, when doubt, difficulty, haters, or the Devil himself comes against us, may we say, "I am doing a great work, and I cannot come down."

EXERCEO DIVINA

Introduction

As I have researched this project over the years, I have become aware that physical well-being is just another aspect of who we are. No one aspect is above the others, but the sum of the parts, working together for God's purposes completes God's calling placed on humanity at creation. The image I have repeatedly gone back to is that of Jesus standing before His accusers, His sentence, and His executioners. I say *image* because our Christ stood before all of them with the same demeanor and conviction: complete submission.

As followers of Jesus, we are attempting, on a daily basis, to model our Messiah's behavior and life. Yet, we often do not truly desire or commit ourselves to those purposes. That is what must end if we ever desire true sanctification: All aspects of ourselves being transformed into the image of Jesus Christ.

How do we get healthier? It is a question we struggle with from time to time. All of us can live healthier in some aspect of our lives: spiritually, mentally, or physically. The connection between the physical, mental, and spiritual realms holds the potential for significantly improving our lives.

The vision of Jesus before His captors is the key for us. For us to be completely transformed by God, we must live our lives in the manner that Jesus did: full submission. By not offering every aspect of who we are to God we are limiting what God can do with us and through us.

Christians must submit every aspect of who they are to Jesus. Clergy and laity alike are called to the same submission. The three components of our humanness are the spiritual, physical, and mental (soul, body, and mind). All of who we are must be offered to God to be used—full submission.

We can no longer reserve part of our lives for sinfulness or overindulgence. It is not acceptable for us to allow vices to rule one portion of our lives. We cannot rationalize excess because we are so good in other parts of our lives or because it is just easier to live apart from God's intentions. The power to overcome our weaknesses lies within us all.

The current instruction in many of our churches is that God is external to us, which is enforced by many, our traditions, and our verbiage, but there is an alternative belief that the *position* of God is inside us. That reality, coupled with the practice of *exerceo divina* and the actual quiet space that I make for God, have made all the difference in my spiritual journey. It is not the voice of a certain expert or a particular health guru that I heard in my head that impacted me so much, but it was the message from God that was finally able to cut through so much clutter than I had padded my brain with that changed me. What a blessing!

Life can push us and guide us into a state of uneasiness, and I know that feeling well. That type of discomfort is the result of grieving the Holy Spirit when we resist the transformation God has for us. Conversely, when we commit ourselves fully to God with reckless abandon, the way Jesus did, we will also find discomfort and uneasiness, initially. Satan and the power of sin can have a strong hold on us, but we can stand against that with God's help. If we allow ourselves to live with that discomfort and experience what it is we need to encounter God in a new and fuller way, God's good work will be completed in us

Now, more than ever, I know God is present in me and working with me. I am trying to make more room for God that one day I will be filled with the perfect love that God is and share that image of Christ with the world around me. Until then, I endeavor to *work the steps* of my spiritual disciplines much as a recovering alcoholic does, because one journey into the dark night was enough for me. God is always there to speak to me if I am able to get out of the way. This program is focused on connecting with God and allowing a holistic wellness to flow out of that. It is my supposition that God has the power to make us healthier spiritually as well as physically and mentally. This program proposes a means to partner with God in that effort; I hope it is beneficial to you.

<u>The Problem</u>

WHERE DOES THE PROPER motivation come from in addressing the issue of physical wellness, specifically fitness and diet? God is all the motivation we need, but our families and loved ones can also inspire us to become more than we are. There are innumerable benefits that can come from making physical wellness a priority: There are quality of life issues, additional years of life, and peace and contentment from doing what you know is the right thing. The possibility does exist that this priority can also bring a person closer to God.

It is quite common in this day and time to focus on diet and exercise. The focus is not done in the manner that would actually be beneficial to society. Rather, it is done in such a way as to exploit the issue and those that suffer from it to insure it is a booming business that will not cease any time soon. There are countless companies and programs designed to generate interest and revenue in the area of physical wellness. There are television advertisements airing throughout regular programming that have *the* way to lose weight with exercise and their *wonder plan*. Celebrities are found promoting a plan that keeps them lean and fit, and they are more than happy to support a plan that provides them with the proper monetary motivation. These miracle plans never address the root of the problem, but they do support the avenues that will maintain this industry for years to come.

Young adults, middle-aged people, and even retired and senior citizens are all target audiences when it comes to these plans. I know many thirty-somethings that are participating in plans designed to boost their metabolisms that are slowing with age. It is as if nature is depriving us of our God-given right to overeat, and we must fight back to defend our indulgences. Conversely, it would seem that we should recognize that food supplies are commodities that should be rationed as earth can only support so many life forms. Our efforts to push the limit of what is acceptable consumption for a person cannot have a happy ending. But no one wants to discuss that possibility, and the insufficient attention to this issue will continue to hurt our ecosystems and all of God's creation.

To further exasperate this problem, people have decided to turn to drugs as an alternative or in combination with physical workout plans and programs. It is not enough that our society is promoting the idea of self-indulgence, but now there are drugs which have a long list of side effects that almost mirror some disorders caused by poor lifestyle choices. The saying, "If the disease doesn't kill you, the cure just might," may ring a little too true in this scenario. Many of these drugs will stimulate customer interest with the *benefit* that their drug or nutritional supplement will help you to see results while allowing you to enjoy "all you care to eat." The irony is not lost on many that all of these remedies fall woefully short of long-term healthy solutions to these weight and exercise issues while not addressing the problem.

These unresolved issues around physical well-being are further supported in our media and visual learning resources with reality television shows like *The Biggest Loser*. The title itself seems to suggest that these contestants are *losers* in society, and the winner is the loser who loses the most weight by percentage of starting weight. This celebration of excess fails to show how many of these contestants are unable to maintain their weight loss after they leave the show. In fact, the track records of these contestants reinforce the underlying theme in this book about self-control. When they no longer have a cadre of physical fitness experts and support structures and the competition of the game show, they are left with themselves and their inability to accept that food is not a way of life, it is a means to support life. Our refusal to endorse this understanding continues to propagate our ignorance and selfishness around the evils that can be a part of food and eating.

To state it simply, we don't want, or like, to be told, "No." We as a part of fallen humanity like things our way, and many of us spend our whole life trying to insure that we are allowed to do what we want to do. Even our scientific understanding of human beings suggests that we like to be in homeostasis, which when you analyze the word, is just a multi-syllable word for being self-possessed. We like to make ourselves happy and keep it that way.

Followers of Christ do not accept fallenness as the goal of creation, and we look to Jesus as the example of how to live life with others before the *self*. Yet many people struggle with this; clergy are no different and are often more guilty of lapses in discipline around food. Without real leadership from the local church on this issue society is suffering. Often, clergy have so many constraints on personal behavior that food becomes a matter of rebellion.

American society is becoming increasingly overweight and unhealthy, which is one reason health insurance costs continue to rise. Even at Asbury Seminary, the break time treats when I began the doctoral program were donuts, cookies, and brownies. Rarely was there a fruit option, and certainly not often enough that it would be perceived as an effort to provide a truly healthy alternative or, more germane to this discussion, provide evidence of the recognition, or acknowledgment, that there is a real problem. Persistence has paid off with the use of evaluation forms and verbal requests because those trends have started to change.

The underlying issue is best summed up by a member of a congregation I served who said when talking about the subject of weight and exercise and fitness, "The truth of the matter is the way to not gain weight as a life plan is to eat less as you get older." Surely that simple plan is not the answer when we desire to do what we want and eat what we want and as much as we want.

There is a tendency to overlook this indiscretion because it is so pervasive and commonplace. Laity and clergy alike should certainly be allowed to enjoy food; after all, it is a harmless vice. This *harmless* addiction has become the number one killer now when linked with the results of years of overeating or unhealthy eating. The pandemic of heart disease, diabetes, and stroke is significant enough as a threat, but this misplaced idolatry can be quite destructive to the spiritual life.

We are all culpable if we ignore the issue of obesity and physical well-being in the Church from the approach of spiritual wholeness and spiritual disciplines. Congregations, composed of pastors and church members, all have parts to play in addressing this issue. Laity has the power to hold clergy accountable and reinforce this concern as an issue that needs to be addressed. Clergy have the authority to work on coordinating the educational programs based in Scripture and spiritual disciplines that can lead the Church towards better lifestyles. Lifestyles that are grounded in wellness and a practical knowledge of physical well-being and scientific insight into general health are possible.

The society as a whole will benefit from this discussion and use of Scripture reading. This emphasis will result in deeper relationships with Christ that will transform the world. This wellness program begins and ends with interaction with God. The goal is to establish how anyone can realize the severity of the effects of overconsumption of food and lack of exercise. With that knowledge, a plan should be implemented that will work to overcome these destructive powers and work toward a union of sound body, mind, and soul.

This is not a program designed to make everyone Ironman triathletes or elite fitness gurus. The idea is to use conventional physical well-being to improve our overall health, and along with that physical well-being, there is a benefit to our spiritual well-being. These factors are interrelated, and one does not guarantee the other.

Working towards wellness as an offering to God may enable one to be a better servant of God and an example that helps others improve their lives as well. Robert Mulholland suggests, "Christian spiritual formation is the process of being conformed to the image of Christ for the sake of others."[56] Spiritual disciplines, specifically Scripture reading, are a means to work on this process of physical wellness. It is not that we are doing these things solely to make ourselves feel better about ourselves or to improve our self-image. There can be collateral benefits to serving God, but our personal agendas are not the motivation needed for true spiritual formation. Those practices can devolve into ego-driven exercises that exist to serve the individual and their agenda, but that cannot be allowed to happen.

The mind-set of spiritual disciplines that are offered to God for the higher purposes of furthering God's message and to God's glory is all the motivation needed. That is how this program is designed to work, and I believe if people commit to it, they will see results that will nourish their spirits and move them to be more like Jesus. We must, however, acknowledge there are problems with individual wellness and look to addressing those issues in our program.

G. Lloyd Rediger addresses the authority that rests on pastors and what they should be doing to work on "body-mind-spirit fitness." Clergy are the ones who are looked to for insight and to establish standards of living a spiritually healthy life, which is dependent on a sound physical as well as spiritual orientation. Rediger provides case studies of pastors who were nearly dysfunctional personally and professionally without some form of exercise regimen and protocol to handle diet and the challenges of pastoral life. Rediger looks to the US Army slogan as a guide for the Church: "[W]e can move ourselves and our parishioners toward the goal of being the best that we can be—under God, and for God's purposes."[57] Traditionally, clergy are in the best situation to help church members with these issues, but we have not utilized that authority.

While needing to exemplify a healthy example to their parishioners, the rigors of life must also be managed. Stress can be a destructive disorder, and its effects can be compounded without adequate exercise and recreation. Our unfitness may not only apply to our own lives and wellness, but it may refer to our ability to serve and function in the world we live.

Diet and food control are the first step to the solution of obesity, but there is more to be done for physical wellness than just regulating the intake of food. Exercise is essential to fighting back against the trends that have become firmly entrenched in the modern life. Roy M. Oswald discusses this scary trend: "The lack of physical exercise is considered by doctors to be the most serious health hazard among North Americans. This includes our children. We have become so sedentary that we are jeopardizing our health."[58] Oswald supports his findings with statistics from the Center for Disease Control: "[R]egular physical exercise reduces the incidence of many medical conditions—and most notably aids in fighting heart disease, colon cancer, diabetes, and obesity."[59] Those illnesses are deadly, and our refusal to address these threats is akin to aiding and abetting a crime by not educating the churches we serve. Oswald does a great deal of seminars and lectures on fitness and wellness, and he touts the additional benefits that I have experienced because of exercise programs: positive emotions after exercise, increased self-esteem, improved fitness, and even aiding sermon preparation.

The Plan

WITH THE AWARENESS OF the reconciliation this new lifestyle can bring, we will now look at what this program is. It is a system of Scripture lessons in concert with exercise and an open and contrite heart that is seeking more than what we can do left to our own without God's presence. The Scripture passages utilized in this program are open to your selection.

The common lectionary is a wonderful tool and useful when attempting to remain disciplined in reading Scripture. If one is attempting to read the Bible over a year, which many churches promote, there is almost too much to be read at one particular prayer session. The Psalms are a great source for introspective material during your devotional time.

Devotional times given unto God, utilizing exercise, provide the foundation for this program. They center and prepare the participant for what needs to be done. It is a time that is helpful in reminding the individual what they are working on and who they are serving. This program enables a person to transition to an incarnational Christian. As followers of Jesus, that is where we are to begin, because from that point we can promote incarnational living. So much of incarnational living takes place outside the church walls, and this program is no different.

Lectio divina is the basis for this program, and that spiritual discipline is described later. Reading Psalms, beginning with the first and moving through the entire collection provides a good structure for *exerceo divina*. One may also choose selected portions of the whole (e.g., the Psalms of Assent: Psalms 120-34). You could also read through the New Testament one chapter at a time. Once the passage is selected, we read the passage and meditate on it using a similar approach to the established discipline of *lectio divina*. What differentiates *exerceo divina* is the time spent passing through *lectio*, *meditatio*, *oratio*, and *contemplatio* while exercising.

In this program, the participant is allowed to listen for God not only while exercising, but he or she is encouraged to search for God in their dietary habits. Exercise and prayer time before meals attempts to focus the individual on what place diet and nutrition have in our lives. So many people suggest that they are unaware when they are overeating or making bad meal selections. They just do not think about the repercussions of the decisions they are making at the dinner table. Appendix 3 offers some strategies to be used at the table, in the buffet line, and in the grocery store.

This program can hopefully raise the participants' awareness and give them the backbone needed to slow down and make good choices. When we stop to listen for God in our spiritual disciplines, whether reading the Bible, praying, or exercising, we can realize that those other idols we worship before God will never fill us the way God's presence can. Fullness is something so many over-eaters never truly find because it is about more than the food.

I was once told by a Benedictine monk in high school that to lose weight all one needed to do was eat the same amount and walk 30 minutes a day. It is simple math really, but it is not always easy for us to make the time. This program makes it a priority.

Many people can keep up with the steps they take every day with their smart watches or phones. People are motivated by competition and meeting their daily walking goals. Not everybody has that motivation, but counting steps is not expensive and can be a useful tool in this program. If walking is what you do best, then walk for God and listen to God while you walk. There is no need to take your phone or iPod along while you exercise. I love a good podcast, but our dependence on having someone's voice in our ears at all times is drowning out one of God's best ways to communicate with you: when you are alone and engaged with creation.

Paul told us to train our bodies and beat them into submission. That process exposes us to God's power and movement, not only making us better but giving us a word to share with others. Pairing exercise with our devotional time provides a solid combination to expand God's reach and presence in our lives and ministry.

Maintaining the distances walked, ran, swam, or cycled, and the foods consumed and the feelings and emotions around this program will be invaluable in getting on the right track. I advise keeping a food and exercise journal, so there is no doubt about your progress and where you are struggling. Some may prefer group exercise, and that can certainly have a place in your weekly routine, but one-on-one time with God is instrumental to the program's success.

Exercise can come in many forms and Appendix 4 details the approach to various forms of exercise that will aid in burning calories and reducing the amount of fat, or stored energy, from body composition. During exercise, the key to remember is that this is being done for God and to become more like Jesus. One must constantly be reminded of the motivation for this program and what is hoped to be gained by participating in it. Incorporating exercise into spiritual disciplines may give people a new approach to battling health issues that have always haunted them.

No challenge is too great for God's grace and power, and I believe if someone truly wants to offer this to God they will be changed. The outside appearance will be impacted, but it is the change on the inside that is most attractive. Loosening the hold that food has on people in our culture of excess can change the way we view other forms of overconsumption and will make significant strides in living lives dependent on God's presence and authority. This program can promote spiritual growth in the individual and be conducive to incarnational living as it impacts the lives of others who learn from it and witness the transformation that is possible through Christ and our commitment to Him.

I do not presume to guarantee that this program will be a panacea that is capable of transforming all who try to incorporate its structure into their lives. A parent who is concerned with physical wellness can influence more than just their family. This program is designed to enable people to present Jesus to the world. People who are struggling with diet and fitness can gain a great deal of benefit from encountering others who are succeeding with the same challenges because of God's presence in them. I believe this program can facilitate that type of transformation.

I have been using *exerceo divina* as a guide, and I have recognized a change in the way I see food and consume it. I continue to use it as a guide on my spiritual journey. Every day is a new day where success and failure are possible, but God is present in me. I can face the challenge and succeed because God is transforming me every day. I know others see my growth, and I witness to the change I have experienced. I pray God's presence continues to fill me and mold me into the image of Jesus for the benefit of the world around me. May others see God's hand at work within me and find the same revelation of who God is that I have been blessed to find.

<u>*Lectio Divina*</u> Format

1. Lectio

-Read the passage slowly and more than once. Try to answer the questions, What is the Bible passage about? What is the context? Who are the main characters? What is God doing in that passage?

2. Meditatio

-Ask, What is God trying to say to me in this Bible passage? The Bible is a living thing, and God speaks to us differently through the Bible at different times in our lives.

3. Oratio

-Pray about what that passage means to your relationship with God. Repeat Samuel's words to God, "Speak, Your servant is listening" (1 Sam. 3:10b), asking God to meet you right there in the words of the Bible passage.

4. Contemplatio

-Remain silent in the presence of God. This is a time to make space for God to tell you something or provide some insight into the Bible passage or your own life.

***All or parts of this approach can be done while exercising

In the Buffet Line

-Always grab a smaller plate when given a choice: studies have shown that smaller plates in buffet lines result in less food being consumed.

-Select only <u>one</u> meat choice in a line.

-Actually think about what you are really hungry for when selecting sides.

-Avoid fried options in the line.

-Do not take more than one type of bread.

-Always prepare a salad and use the low fat and low sugar option: salad should be helping your diet not making it unhealthier.

-Choose an unprocessed fruit alternative to refined sugar desserts.

At a Restaurant

-If you are served a meal, ask for a to-go box at the beginning of the meal: divide the meal up so you can have another meal later in the week.

-Focus your attention on the person you are dining with and strive for conversation time: it will slow down the meal and allow you to be aware of what you are eating and to feel full sooner.

At the Dinner Table

-Always begin your meal with quiet and a prayer asking God for strength as you eat to avoid over-consuming. You may even choose to pray for guidance before you order to avoid an unhealthy food choice.

<u>In the Grocery Store</u>

-Always have a list prepared before you shop and stick to the list.

-Plan your trips to the store after a meal or a snack: this limits the compulsion buying that is so prevalent in grocery stores. Grocers design their stores to encourage compulsion purchases, which are almost always unhealthy and overpriced.

All exercise is to be done with a doctor's approval.

Walking

-John Wesley stated that walking was the ideal form of exercise, and I am not one to normally disagree with Father Wesley, so I will not start now. It is a form of conveyance that is drastically underutilized and will be beneficial to this program. It is particularly helpful for those who are physically limited in which forms of exercise they can participate.

-Walking should be done in such a manner as to elevate the heart rate for the amount of time designated for exercise.

-Be aware of where you are and what you are doing, but allow your consciousness to connect with God.

-Begin your walks with the passage of Scripture you most recently read in your mind (e.g., from the daily office or a devotion).

-Say a prayer of illumination as you start—inviting God to meet you in that moment, and wait expectantly for God's connection with you.

Running

-Running requires a little more awareness of your surroundings if you are around cars, bikes, or other runners.

-You should begin with Scripture and a prayer.

-The target is an elevated heart rate beyond a conversational pace, but it is still an endeavor with great potential for an encounter with God.

Cycling

-Cycling requires more awareness of your surroundings than walking or running because of the speed at which you travel and the increased chance of injury.

- You should begin with Scripture and a prayer.

-I have found cycling requires more attention to pace when attempting to elevate the heart rate as it is an "easier" and more efficient way to move the body.

Swimming

-I prefer swimming in the pool to open water as there are fewer unseen dangers (e.g., animals and foreign objects).

-You should begin with Scripture and a prayer.

-Swimming is a great workout as it does not put as much pressure on the knees and it engages all of the major muscle groups in the body.

Gym Training (Cardiovascular Machines)

-There are numerous ways to exercise at a local gym that simulate exercise outdoors (e.g., treadmill, elliptical, rowing).

-The same rules apply from the other cardiovascular exercises. The focus and the manner of engaging God is similar, but the setting is different. The threat of injury from traffic and others is decreased, but caution should be used when using such powerful equipment.

-Weight bearing exercises (push-ups, etc.) strengthen the joints and promote muscle tone and development.

-Weight bearing exercises are beneficial to exercise programs, but it is harder to concentrate on God because of the raised awareness of others and the attention needed to adjust to the start/stop nature of the exercises.

-Personal trainers are valuable assets at gyms to help participants design a program that is safe and effective. They should be consulted before any weight training is initiated.

ACKNOWLEDGEMENTS

I FIRST WANT TO THANK my wife Lindsey for her love, devotion, and encouragement over the years it took me to complete this book. You were always an affirming and motivating voice who had to show some tough love by lighting a gentle (or not so gentle) fire or two under me to keep me on task. You were patient…for the most part, and I appreciate you more than you will ever know…and not just because of your final edit on this book. I love you and depend on you and thank God for you every day!

I want to thank my children, Hannah and Joseph, for allowing Daddy to disappear into his *cloffice* to work on this book more times than I care to think about or mention. Hannah, you will be a great writer one day, and I hope seeing and reading this book will motivate you to work on your craft. Joseph, you are my exercise buddy, and I enjoy our times on the road together as such special moments. I expect great things from your problem-solving mind. I love you both, so, so much!

I am so thankful for my parents, Joe and Marilyn, who are career educators. They taught me to love learning and helping others learn. Thank you, Dad, for always believing in me even when you did not understand why I was doing what I was doing. Mom, you were my first editor in life, and you never held back. Thank you for teaching me to have high standards in my writing and how valuable a rough draft is. To both of you, "I love you the best."

ENDNOTES

1 David Stoop, *Living with a Perfectionist* (Nashville: Oliver-Nelson, 1987), Print.

2 Kenneth L. Barker and John R. Kohlenberger, III, *Zondervan NIV Bible Commentary. Vol. 1 Premier reference series* (Grand Rapids: Zondervan, 1994), Print, 99.

3 Ibid.

4 Maxie Dunman and Kimberly Dunnam Reisman, *The Workbook on the 7 Deadly Sins* (Nashville: Upper Room, 1997), Print, 160-61.

5 Ibid., 163.

6 Ibid., 106.

7 Ibid., 113.

8 Thomas Coke and Francis Asbury, Foreword. *Primitive Physick: Or, an Easy and Natural Method of Curing Most Diseases* (Bristol, N.p., 1765), *Google Book Search*, Web, 23 June 2012, xi.

9 Randy L. Maddox, *Responsible Grace: John Wesley's Practical Theology* (Nashville: Kingswood, 1994), Print, 145.

10 John Wesley, *Primitive Physick: Or, an Easy and Natural Method of Curing Most Diseases* (Bristol: N.p., 1765), *Google Book Search*, Web, 23 June 2012, x.

11 Ibid., iii.

12 Maddox, *Responsible Grace*, 146.

13 Ibid., 147.

14 Wesley, *Primitive Physick*, iv.

15 Ibid.

16 Ibid., vi.

17 Ibid., viii.

18 Ibid., ix.

19 John Piper, "116 Been Real," Desiring God, Desiring God, 6 October 2017, https://www.desiringgod.org/articles/116-been-real.

20 Wesley, *Primitive Physick*, vi.

21 Maddox, *Responsible Grace*, 215.

22 Wesley, *Primitive Physick*, vii.

23 Maddox, *Responsible Grace*, 216.

24 Charles Yrigoyen, Jr., *John Wesley: Holiness of Heart and Life* (New York: General Board of Global Ministries, the United Methodist Church, 1996), Print, 47.

25 Joseph A. Buck, IV, "Improving United Methodist Clergy Wellness through Exercise and Scripture Reading," (D.Min. diss., Asbury Theological Seminary, 2012), 111.

26 Deepta Gate, William Brooks, Bernard E. McCarey, and Henry F. Edelhauser, "Pharmacokinetics of Intraocular Drug Delivery by Periocular Injections Using Ocular Fluorophotometry," National Library of Medicine, pubmed.gov, 27 September 2010, https://pubmed.ncbi.nlm.nih.gov/17460284/.

27 Ray S. Anderson, *On Being Human: Essays in Theological Anthropology* (Grand Rapids: Eerdmans, 1982), Print, 132.

28 Gregory A. Boyd and Paul R. Eddy, *Across the Spectrum: Understanding Issues in Evangelical Theology* (Grand Rapids: Baker Academic, 2002), Print, 88-100.

29 Destin, Sandlin, "The Backwards Brain Bicycle," Smarter Every Day, YouTube, 24 April 2015, https://www.youtube.com/watch?v=MFzDaBzBlL0.

30 Robert M. Mulholland, Jr., *Shaped by the Word: The Power of Scripture in Spiritual Formation* (Nashville: Upper Room, 1985), Print, 29.

31 Anderson, *On Being Human*, 133.

32 E. A. Livingstone, *The Concise Oxford Dictionary of the Christian Church*, 2ⁿᵈ ed. (New York: Oxford UP, 2000), Print, 456.

33 Cheslyn Jones, Geoffrey Wainwright, and Edward Yarnold, eds., *The Study of Spirituality* (New York: Oxford UP, 1986), Print, 96-99.

34 Anderson, *On Being Human*, 133.

35 Rudolf Bultmann, *Theology of the New Testament*. Trans. Kendrick Grobel. 1 Vol. (New York: Scribner's, 1955), Print, 192-201.

36 Brown, Warren S., Nancey Murphy, and H. Newton Malony, eds., *Whatever Happened to the Soul? Scientific and Theological Portraits of Human Nature* (Minneapolis: Fortress, 1998), Print, 163-65.

37 Max Martin, Karl Johan Schuster, and Taylor Swift, "Shake It Off," Recorded 2013, Track Six on *1989*, Big Machine, Compact Disc.

38 "Flint," Wikipedia: https://en.wikipedia.org/wiki/Flint, 1 November 2019.

39 *The Patriot*, directed by Roland Emmerich (2000; Culver City, CA: Columbia Pictures/Centropolis Entertainment/Mutual Film Company), Theater.

40 *Lord of the Rings: The Fellowship of the Ring*, directed by Peter Jackson (2002; Burbank, CA: New Line Cinema), DVD.

41 David M. Hale, "The Unbelievable Tales of LSU Head Coach Ed Orgeron," ESPN, https://www.espn.com/college-football/story/_/id/28434335/the-unbelievable-tales-lsu-head-coach-ed-orgeron, 8 January 2020.

42 *The Karate Kid Part II*, directed by John G. Avildsen (1986; Los Angeles, CA: Columbia Pictures), Theater.

43 Jack Zimmerman, "Sukkot, the Feast of Booths," Jewish Voice, 1 December 2015, https://www.jewishvoice.org/read/blog/sukkot-the-feast-of-booths-known-to-some-as-the-feast-of-tabernacles.

44 Malcolm Gladwell, *Outliers: The Story of Success* (New York: Back Bay Books. 2008) Print, 38.

45 Ibid., 41.

46 *The Godfather*, Directed by Francis Ford Coppola (1972; Hollywood, CA: Paramount Pictures), DVD.

47 Wallace J. Nichols, *Blue Mind: The Surprising Science That Shows How Being Near, In, On, or Under Water Can Make You Happier, Healthier, More Connected, and Better at What You Do* (New York: Back Bay Books, 2014), Print, 215.

48 Ibid.

49 Ibid.

50 Ibid., 217.

51 Ibid., 218-219.

52 Jon Deak, "Laughing Chewbacca Mask Lady," OneSixthSociety, YouTube, 19 May 2016, https://www.youtube.com/watch?v=y3yRv5Jg5TI.

53 Robert Burns, (1786). Poems, Chiefly in the Scottish Dialect (First ed.), Kilmarnock: Printed for John Wilson, Retrieved 26 January 2016 via Internet Archive.

54 "NFL Playcall: How Hard Can It Be?" Wall Street Journal, YouTube, 26 January 2015, https://www.youtube.com/watch?v=bHLrXMPBQ9s.

55 *Anchorman: The Legend of Ron Burgundy*, directed by Adam McKay (2004; Los Angeles, CA: Apatow Productions/DreamWorks Pictures), Theater.

56 Mulholland, Jr., *Shaped by the Word*, 25.

57 G. Lloyd Rediger, *Fit to Be a Pastor* (Louisville: Westminster-Knox Press, 2000), Print, 12.

58 Roy M. Oswald, *Clergy Self-Care: Finding a Balance for Effective Ministry.* (New York: Alban Institute, 1991), Print, 141.

59 Ibid., 141.

CPSIA information can be obtained
at www.ICGtesting.com
Printed in the USA
BVHW040848040322
630664BV00011B/152